Robert J. Dixson

Easy Reading Selections in English

For Intermediate Level

With Drills in Conversation Based on the Reading Selections

DISAL EDITORA

Assistente editorial: Gabriela Canato
Capa: Alberto Mateus

Dados Internacionais de Catalogação na Publicação (CIP)
(Câmara Brasileira do Livro, SP, Brasil)

Easy reading selections in English : with drills in conversation based on the reading selections / by Robert J. Dixson. -- Barueri, SP : DISAL, 2007.

Vários autores
ISBN 978-85-89533-88-1

1. Inglês - Livros-texto para estrangeiros 2. Leitura I. Dixson, Robert James.

07-9437 CDD-428

Índice para catálogo sistemático:
1. Inglês para brasileiros : Lingüística aplicada 428

DISAL EDITORA

Al. Mamoré, 911 - sala 107, Alphaville
06454-040, Barueri - SP
Tel./Fax: **55 11 4195-2811**

Visite nosso site: www.disaleditora.com.br

VENDAS
Televendas: (11) 3226-3111
Fax gratuito: 0800 7707 105/106
E-mail para pedidos: comercialdisal@disal.com.br

FOREWORD

This book will provide easy reading selections for students on the intermediate level of learning English. The selections are simplified versions of well-known stories by classic authors, and should offer no difficulty to those who have completed the elementary phases in the study of English. The book can be used in the second six months of study, or as a general reader in the second year course, depending, naturally, on the degree of advancement of the student or class.

For students not sufficiently advanced, the following texts by the author are recommended as preparation for this book: "Beginning Lessons in English," and "Exercises in English Conversation." The text entitled "Graded Exercises in English" may also be used as a general grammar supplement to this book. In any case, the stories here presented should not be attempted until the student is adequately prepared. Otherwise, studying the text becomes a tedious exercise in translation, rather than the pleasure that is experienced in reading what is readily understood. Exercises follow each selection in the form of questions. The answers which these questions evoke provide excellent conversation material for the student.

For further suggestions as to the use of these exercises for conversational purposes, see the foreword to the text "Exercises in English Conversation." The question exercises in this text follow the same general plan as those used in the conversation book, and should be used with the same objectives in view. This book, in effect, may be considered as a second conversation book as well as a reader, to be used upon completion of the elementary conversation book. In general, the questions should be supplemented wherever possible by questions of a similar nature or theme. The questions should be altered to suit the particular class situation. Personal names or facts can be substituted in order to give a more natural and life-like quality to the material. The teacher should introduce much repetition and should require of students direct, complete and automatic answers. If answers are slow or hesitant, questions should be repeated several times, or more home preparation demanded, until the desired fluency or control is obtained.

Robert J. Dixson

CONTENTS

THE CHRISTMAS PRESENT

O. Henry

PART I

One dollar and eighty-seven cents. That was all. And sixty cents of it was in pennies. Pennies which Della had saved one at a time. Three times Della counted it. One dollar and eighty-seven cents. And the next day would be Christmas.

While Della is crying in this way, let us take a look at the home in which she lives. It is a small furnished apartment at eight dollars a week, and it is a very poor one. Everywhere there are signs of poverty.

Della finished crying, got up, and began to powder her face. She stood by the window and looked out with little interest at a gray cat walking along a gray fency in a gray back yard. Tomorrow would be Christmas day, and she had only $1.87 with which to buy Jim, her husband, a present. She had been saving every penny she could for months with this result. Twenty dollars a week doesn't go far. Expenses had been greater than she expected. They always are. Only $1.87 to buy a present for Jim. She had spent many happy hours planning for something nice for him, something fine and rare, something worthy of the honor of being owned by Jim.

There was a narrow mirror between the windows of the room. Suddenly Della turned from the window and stood before the mirror. Her eyes suddenly began to shine brilliantly, although her face turned a little pale. Rapidly she pulled down her hair and let it fall to its full length.

Now, there were two possessions in which Jim and Della took great pride. One was Jim's gold watch, that had previously been his father's and, before that, his grandfather's. The other was Della's beautiful hair, which now fell about her shoulders like a beautiful cascade of water. It reached below her knees. Quickly, now, she combed it again and arranged it properly. She hesitated for a moment and tears appeared in her eyes.

She put on her old brown coat. She put on her old brown hat. With her eyes shining, she flew out of the room and down the stairs to the street.

She walked some distance and finally stopped at a shop with a sign which read: "Madame Sofronio, Hair Goods of All Kinds." Della ran up the stairs to the second floor where the shop was located. She was breathing heavily.

"Will you buy my hair?" asked Della.

"I buy hair," said Madame. "Take your hat off and let me have a look at it."

Della removed her hat and let fall her beautiful hair.

"Twenty dollars," said Madame, feeling the hair with her experienced hand.

"Give it to me quickly," said Della.

PART II

The next two hours flew by quickly. She was busy looking everywhere in the stores for Jim's present.

She found it at last. It surely had been made for Jim and for no one else. There was no other like it in any of the stores and she had been everywhere. It was a platinum watch chain, a beautiful one, worthy of the Watch. As soon as she saw it she knew that it must be for Jim. It was like him, good taste and quality. The description applied to both. It cost twenty-one dollars. Della hurried home with the eighty-seven cents which remained.

When Della arrived home she was less excited, and gradually she became more reasonable. She began to comb and arrange her hair, now cut very short, in the best way she could. She took her curling iron and began to curl her hair carefully. Then she looked at herself in the mirror critically. "If Jim doesn't kill me," she said to herself, "before he looks at me a second time, he'll say that I look like a child. But what could I do with only a dollar and eighty-seven cents?"

At seven o'clock the coffee was made and the dinner almost ready.

Jim was never late. Della held the chain in her hand and sat on the corner of the table near the door. Then she heard his step on the stairs and for a moment she turned white.

The door opened and Jim stepped in and closed it. He looked thin and serious. Poor fellow, he was only twenty-two, and he had all the problems of having a family. He needed a new overcoat, and he was without gloves.

Jim's eyes were fixed upon Della, and there was suddenly an expression in them that she could not read, and it frightened her. He simply looked at her with a strange expression.

Della jumped off the table and went toward him.

"Jim, darling," she said, "don't look at me in that way. I had my hair cut off and I sold it because I wanted to give you a Christmas present. My hair will grow again — you don't mind, do you? I simply had to do it. My hair grows very fast. Say 'Merry Christmas' to me, Jim, and let's be happy. You don't know what a nice — what a beautiful gift I bought for you."

PART III

"You have cut off your hair," Jim said, as though he could not possibly understand.

"I cut it off and sold it," said Della. "Don't you like me just as well? I am the same person without my hair."

Jim looked around the room curiously.

"You say that your hair is gone?" he said, with an air almost of foolishness.

"It is not necessary to look for it," said Della. 'It's sold, I tell you — sold and gone. It's Christmas evening, darling. So be good to me — because I sold my hair for you."

Jim seemed suddenly to wake up. He kissed Della. Then he took a package out of his pocket and threw it upon the table.

"Don't make any mistake, Della," he said, "about me. Nothing that could ever happen would ever make me think less of you."

Her white fingers quickly undid the package. And then a cry of joy — and next a quick feminine change to tears and crying.

For there lay the combs, the set of combs, side and back, that Della had admired for such a long time in a Broadway store window. They were beautiful combs — just the color to go with her beautiful hair. And now they were hers, but the hair in which she was to wear them was gone.

But at last she was able to smile through her tears and say, "My hair grows so fast, Jim."

And then Della jumped up like a little cat and cried, "Oh, Oh!"

Jim had not yet seen his beautiful present, the new chain for his watch. She held it out to him anxiously in her hand.

"Isn't it a fine one, Jim? I hunted all over town to find it. You'll have to look at your watch a hundred times a day now to find out the time. Give me your watch. I want to see how it looks on it."

Instead of obeying, Jim lay down on the couch and put his hands under the back of his head and smiled.

"Della," said he, "let's put our Christmas presents away and keep them awhile. They are too nice to use at present. I sold my watch in order to get the money to buy your combs. And now perhaps you can get dinner ready."

Exercises Based on

THE CHRISTMAS PRESENT

PART I

A. Answer These Questions:

1. Had Della saved much or little money for Jim's present? 2. Was the money which she had saved all in pennies, nickels or quarters? 3. What holiday was approaching? 4. What are the most important holidays in the United States? 5. What are the most important holidays in your native country? 6. Which day of the year is Independence Day in the United States? 7. On which day of the week does Thanksgiving Day always fall? 8. Why had Della been able to save

very little money for Jim's present? 9. Who was Jim? 10. Was Jim's salary large or small? 11. In general, would you consider Della economical or extravagant? 12. What were the two possessions in which Della and Jim took great pride? 13. Why were they so proud of Della's hair? 14. To whom had Jim's watch belonged previously? 15. What kind of watch have you, a pocket watch or a wrist watch? 16. Does your watch ordinarily run slow or fast? 17. How often do you wind your watch? 18. To what shop did Della go after deciding to sell her hair? 19. Was this shop located on the first or the second floor? 20. How many floors are there in the school building in which you study English?

B. Vocabulary Drill. Choose The Correct Form:

1. *Narrow* is the opposite of (big, little, wide, deep).
2. A *penny* is (five cents, one cent, two cents, half a dollar).
3. The word *sign* is pronounced to rhyme with (lion, line, seen, been).
4. Distinguish in meaning between *pale* and *pail.*
5. Give the corresponding noun form of these adjectives: *long, wide, high, deep.*
6. The word *knees* is pronounced to rhyme with (niece, peace, sneeze, face).
7. Give the past tense form and the past participle form of these verbs: *run, step, put, fly, buy, take, feel, give.*
8. Which of these words is not spelled correctly: *previeusly, possession, shining, experienced?*
9. Give the opposites of these words: *heavy, old, beautiful, full, below, poor, far, happy.*
10. A common synonym for *finally* is (at first, at hand, at last, seldom).

C. Use These In Sentences:

to take a look at, to get up, to look out, to go far, to let something fall, to take pride in, for a moment, to put on, in general.

PART II

A. Answer These Questions:

1. What present did Della finally choose for Jim? 2. Was the present made of gold, silver or platinum? 3. Is platinum scarce or plentiful? 4. Of what material is your watch made? 5. Are gold watches generally more expensive or less expensive than watches made of silver? 6. Was the chain which Della bought for Jim a cheap one or an expensive one? 7. Which keep better time, cheap watches or expensive watches? 8. Which have a finer mechanism, cheap watches or expensive watches? 9. Was Della calm or excited when she arrived home with Jim's present? 10. Was her hair now short or long? 11. Do most women today wear their hair short or long? 12. What did Della begin to do with her curling iron? 13. Do you have curly or straight hair? 14. What is the difference between curly hair and wavy hair? 15. Why did Della turn white when she heard Jim's step on the stairs? 16. Does the fact that Jim was poorly dressed indicate that they were rich or poor? 17. Was Jim young or old? 18. Did he earn much or little? 19. What reason did Della give Jim for cutting off her hair? 20. Had Della cut her hair off in order to buy Jim a birthday present or a Christmas present?

B. Vocabulary Drill. Choose The Correct Form:

1. A synonym for *quickly* is (seen, seldom, rapidly, slowly).
2. A synonym for *surely* is (sometimes, certainly, frequently, nicely).
3. *Gradually* means (now and then, little by little, rarely, quickly).
4. The word *comb* is pronounced to rhyme with (come, some, tomb, home, thumb).
5. Give the past tense form and the past participial form of these verbs: *cut, take, say, hold, need, look, have, buy, know, make.*
6. Which of these past tense forms are pronounced as words of one syllable and which are pronounced as words of two syllables: *looked, turned, stepped, wanted, needed, closed, fixed?*
7. To *mind* something is to (like it, have some objection to it, describe it, need it).
8. Give the opposites of these words: *last, everywhere, less, short, best, carefully, late, thin, new, fast.*

9. In which of these words is the letter *s* pronounced like *s* and in which is it pronounced like *z*: *busy, is, else, was, cents, fast, does, gloves?*

10. Use each of these words in sentences, once as a noun and once as a verb: *watch, taste, mind, chain, curl, comb, cost, present.*

C. Use These In Sentences:

to fly by, to look for, at last, no one else, as soon as, to look at, to look like, to turn white, to step in (out), to jump off.

PART III

A. Answer These Questions:

1. Was Jim pleased or displeased when he saw Della with short hair? 2. What had happened to Della's hair? 3. On what night of the year did all this happen? 4. What do people usually do on New Year's Eve in the United States? 5. What special customs, if any, are followed in your country on New Year's Eve? 6. What do you usually do on Christmas Day in your country? 7. Where did you spend last Christmas Day? 8. What Christmas present had Jim bought for Della? 9. Did Della laugh or cry when she undid the package? 10. Where had Della seen the combs previously? 11. Why was Della now unable to wear the combs? 12. Why did the fact that Della's hair grew fast give her some consolation? 13. What present did Della now give Jim? 14. Was the present which Della gave Jim useful or useless to him? 15. Why was the present useless to him? 16. Do you consider it useless or useful to study foreign languages? 17. What foreign language besides English have you studied? 18. In your opinion, how long does it take to learn to speak a foreign language well? 19. Do you find this story interesting or dull? 20. Do the characters of this story seem to you real or unreal?

B. Vocabulary Drill. Choose The Correct Form:

1. A cry of *joy* is a cry of (pain, happiness, disappointment, surprise).

2. Distinguish in meaning between *to cut up something* and *to cut off something.*

3. What is the corresponding adjective form of the verb *to obey?* What is the corresponding noun form?

4. A synonym for *perhaps* is (always, sometimes, of course, maybe).

5. Give the past tense form and the past participial form of these verbs: *obey, sell, cut, throw, make.*

6. To *undo* a package is to (throw it away, lose it, hide it, unwrap or untie it).

7. The word *could* is pronounced to rhyme with (cold, pulled, good, soiled).

8. Give the opposites of these: *to wake up, to sit down, to get up.*

9. A synonym for *at present* is (soon, later, now, a little while ago).

10. Which one of these words is not spelled correctly: *feminine, beautiful, Cristmas, obeying, anxiously?*

C. Use These In Sentences:

to cut off, to look around, to look for, to wake up, to take out, to go with, to be able (unable), to jump up, to find out.

THE STOLEN LETTER

Edgar Allan Poe

PART I

At Paris, just after dark one evening in the autumn of 18 - -, I was enjoying the company of an old friend, C. Auguste Dupin, in his small library. The door of the room was opened suddenly and an old acquaintance, Monsieur G., head of the Paris police, entered.

We were glad to see him, for we had not seen him for several years. Monsieur G. said that he had come to consult us, or rather to ask the opinion of my friend Dupin, about some official business which was causing him a great deal of trouble.

"I will tell you in a few words what it is," he said, "but

before I begin, let me tell you that this is a matter of the greatest secrecy and I might lose my position if it became known that I had told someone about it."

"Proceed," said I.

"Well, I have received confidential information that a document of great importance has been stolen from the royal apartments. The thief is Minister D - -. The person from whom the letter was stolen needs the letter badly. But, of course, he cannot proceed openly. And he has asked me to take care of the problem."

"My first act," he went on, "was to make a careful inspection of the minister's apartment. Of course, I had to do this secretly and without his knowledge because we do not want the minister to know that we suspect him. Fortunately, the daily habits of the minister helped me greatly. He is frequently absent from home at night. He has only a few servants and they do not sleep in his apartment. I have keys, as you know, with which I can open any door in Paris. For three months, a night has not passed in which I have not been busy personally searching his apartment. It is now a question of my honor and my reputation. In addition, to mention a great secret, the reward is enormous. Therefore I did not discontinue the search until I was completely satisfied that the thief is a more clever man than I am. I am sure that I have examined every corner of the apartment in which it is possible that the paper can be hidden."

"But is it not possible," I suggested, "that although the minister has the letter, he has hidden it somewhere outside the apartment?"

"Oh, no!" said the police officer. "Twice he has been stopped on the street by my own men, pretending to be thieves, and thev have searched him carefully under my own inspection."

"Tell us," said I, "exactly what you did in your search of the apartment."

"I have had long experience in these matters," answered the police officer. "Thus, I examined the apartment room by room, spending an entire week in each room. We examined the furniture. We opened every drawer, and I suppose you know that for an experienced police officer such a thing as a secret drawer is impossible. Next, we examined the chairs. We removed the tops from all the tables."

"But," I said, "you were not able to take apart all the pieces of furniture. That would be impossible."

"Of course," he answered. "But we did better. We examined every section of each piece of furniture under a very powerful microscope — and we found no indications or marks that the furniture had been touched or disturbed in any way to create a hiding place for the letter. After we had examined the furniture, we examined the apartment itself. We divided the entire surface into sections, and gave a number to each section so that we could not possibly miss any. Then we inspected each square inch of the apartment."

PART II

"You examined the grounds around the house?"

"Yes — but that gave us little trouble. The grounds are paved with bricks. We examined each brick and also the grass between the bricks and found no indication that anything had been touched or moved."

"You looked among the minister's papers, of course, and into the books of his library?"

"Certainly, we opened every package. We not only opened every book but turned every page in each volume. We also inspected carefully the cover of each book with our miscroscope."

"You examined the floors beneath the carpets?"

"Certainly! We removed every carpet and examined every

board beneath the carpets."

"And the paper on the walls?"

"Yes."

"You looked in the cellar?"

"We did."

"Then," I said, "you have been making a mistake, and the letter is not in the apartment."

"I am afraid you are right," said the officer. "And now, Dupin, what would you advise me to do?"

"I would advise you to make a second careful search of the apartment," said Dupin.

"But I am sure the letter is not in the apartment," said the officer.

"I have no better advice to give you," said Dupin. "Of course, you have an accurate description of the letter."

"Oh, yes," said the officer. Then, producing a memorandum book, he began to read aloud a detailed description of the missing letter. Soon afterward he left, more sad in spirit than I had ever seen him before.

About a month later he visited us again. We were seated in the library as before.

"Well, what about the missing letter?" I asked him after he had taken a chair. "I suppose you have decided at last that the minister is too clever to be caught."

"Damn it, yes," he said. "I examined the apartment again, as Dupin suggested but without success."

"How much money has been offered as the reward?" asked Dupin.

"A great deal," he said. "In fact, the amount has been doubled recently. But if it were three times as much I couldn't do anything more toward finding the letter. But I will say this — that I will give my personal check for fifty thousand francs to anyone who gets that letter for me."

"In that case," said Dupin, opening a drawer and producing a checkbook, "you can write me a check for that amount. When you have signed the check, I will give you the letter."

Both the police officer and I were greatly surprised. For a moment the officer remained speechless, but then recovering himself, he picked up a pen and wrote a check for fifty thousand francs and handed it to Dupin. Dupin examined the check carefully and then put it into his pocket. Then he unlocked a drawer and took out a letter and gave it to the police officer. It was the stolen letter. The police officer accepted it with trembling hand. He read its contents hurriedly and then rushed from the room and from the house. When he had gone Dupin began to explain to me how he had gotten the letter.

PART III

"I knew the minister in question very well," he said. "He is a mathematician and a poet — and also a very clever and daring man. I knew that such a man would be familiar with all the usual actions of the police and that he would prepare himself against them. His frequent absences from home at night were only a trick in my estimation. He knew that the police would search every corner of his apartment, and so he permitted them to do it freely. I saw that as a result of all this he would be forced to do something very simple.

"But this is a point, it appears, somewhat above or below the understanding of the police. The police officer, for example, never suspected that it was possible that the minister had placed the letter clearly under the nose of everybody in order to prevent anyone from seeing it.

"Full of these ideas, I put on a pair of black glasses and went to visit the minister one fine morning in his apartment. I told him that my eyes were very weak and that, therefore, I had to wear dark glasses. But with my black glasses I was able to inspect the whole apartment without his noticing the movement of my eyes. Finally, I noticed a small box in full view on the mantelpiece. In this box there were five or six visiting cards and a letter. The letter was very dirty and was torn across the middle. It had been put carelessly into one of the sections of the box. As soon as I saw the letter, I was sure it was the one I was looking for. Certainly it was in appearance different from the original letter. The address on the envelope was different; the handwriting on the envelope had also been changed and was small and feminine in form as if the letter had been written by a woman. But the size was the same. All these things, full in the view of every visitor to the apartment, made me suspicious. I examined the letter as carefully as I could without the minister's noticing me, and it was clear to me that the letter had been turned inside out, like a glove, and re-addressed and changed slightly. I later said good-bye to the minister but left my cigarette case on the table intentionally.

"The next morning I called upon him again to get my cigarette case. We began to converse again, but suddenly there was a pistol shot in the street. D - - - - - rushed to the window and remained there several minutes looking into the street. Really, it was all part of my plan. One of my own men had fired the shot in order to attract attention. Anyway, while D - - - - - was busy at the window, I stepped to the mantelpiece, took the letter, and replaced it with an exact copy which I had prepared at home and brought with me."

"But why did you replace the letter with a copy? Why didn't you take the letter openly on your first visit and leave?"

"D - - - - - is a clever and dangerous man," Dupin replied. "There are many men in the house whom he employs. If I had done the foolish thing which you suggest it is possible I would never have left the place alive and the good people of Paris would never have heard of me again."

Exercises Based on

THE STOLEN LETTER

PART I

A. Answer These Questions:

1. In what city does this story take place? 2. Is Paris the capital of France or the capital of England? 3. What is the native language of the people of Paris? 4. Was Monsieur G. head of the Paris police or head of the London police? 5. What was Monsieur G's purpose in coming to visit Monsieur Dupin? 6. Was the matter which he had come to discuss one of great secrecy or one of little secrecy? 7. What had been stolen from the royal apartments? 8. Was the thief who had stolen the document known or unknown to the police? 9. Was the first act of the police officer to make a very quick or a very careful search of the minister's apartment? 10. Why had the search of the apartment been made very secretly? 11. Did the daily habits of the minister and his frequent absences from home help the police a great deal or very little? 12. Did the minister have few servants or many servants? 13. Was the reward which was offered enormous or very small? 14. Why did the police twice stop the minister on the street? 15. When the police stopped the minister on the street, what did they pretend to be? 16. Why did the police use a microscope in their examination of the furniture? 17. Does a microscope make things look larger or smaller? 18. Did the police officer say that he had had much experience or little experience in such matters? 19. Why did the police divide the surface of the room into sections and give each section a number? 20. Were the police successful or unsuccessful in their search of the apartment?

B. Vocabulary Drill. Choose The Correct Form:

1. *A great deal* means (a little, a lot, a short time, a long time).
2. Distinguish in meaning between *acquaintance* and *friend.*
3. A synonym for *fortunately* is (gladly, frequently, luckily, by chance).

4. The word *drawer* is pronounced to rhyme with (far, store, near, under).

5. The opposite of *to take apart* is to (put away, put together, put off, call off).

6. Give the opposites of these words: outside, powerful, long, possible, better, dark, few, lose, open, careful, absent.

7. *Enormous* means (small, difficult, rather large, very large).

8. Distinguish in meaning and pronunciation between *lose* and *loose*.

9. A synonym for *frequently* is (seen, often, rarely, rapidly).

10. Give the plural form of these nouns: thief, wife, knife, key, library.

C. Use These In Sentences:

to cause trouble, to become known, to take care of, to make a search, at night, in addition, room by room, to take apart.

PART II

A. Answer These Questions:

1. Were the police successful or unsuccessful in their search of the grounds around the house? 2. Were the grounds around the house paved with bricks or with cement? 3. Did the police find anything among the minister's papers or were they unsuccessful here again? 4. Why did the police again use their microscope to examine the library books? 5. What success did the police have in their examination of the carpets and the paper on the walls? 6. Did the police limit their search to the minister's rooms or did they also look in the cellar of the house? 7. Did Dupin advise the police officer to give up the search or to search the apartment a second time? 8. What is the difference between the words *advise* and *advice*? 9. Did the police officer have a general or a detailed description of the missing letter in his memorandum book? 10. Did he keep this description secret or did he read it aloud to his two friends? 11. Was the police officer happy in spirit or sad in spirit when he left his two friends? 12. Was it a month later or a year later when he returned to ask Dupin's advice? 13. Had the police officer been successful or unsuccessful meanwhile

in his second search of the apartment? 14. Was the minister who had stolen the letter apparently a very stupid or a very clever fellow? 15. Had the reward been increased or reduced in the meantime? 16. Was the personal check which the police officer gave to Dupin one of large amount or one of small amount? 17. After Dupin received the check, what did he take from the drawer and give the police officer? 18. Did the police officer accept the letter with a steady or with a trembling hand? 19. When a person is very cold, does he tremble or does he shiver? 20. Did the police officer read the letter slowly or did he read the contents hurriedly and then rush from the room?

B. Vocabulary Drill. Choose The Correct Form:

1. A common synonym for *beneath* is (ever, beyond, under, through).

2. A *board* is made of (paper, wood, brick, cement, plastic).

3. Which of these different parts of a house might be considered as the opposite of the *cellar* (roof, living room, attic, first floor, porch)?

4. Distinguish in use between the words *advise* and *advice*.

5. Give the corresponding noun form of these verbs: describe, examine, suppose, remain, produce, explain.

6. To *tremble* is to (hesitate, shake, draw back, look surprised).

7. To do something *hurriedly* is to do it (with care, slowly, on time, rapidly).

8. The word *damn* is pronounced to rhyme with (dumb, lamb, came, come).

9. To *unlock* something, you generally need a (pen, knife, checkbook, key).

10. Give the past tense form and the past participial form of these verbs: find, touch, do, make, advise, begin, read, leave, see, double, get, write.

C. Use These In Sentences:

to look into, to make a mistake, to be right, to read aloud, at last, a great deal, to pick up, to take out.

PART III

A. Answer These Questions:

1. Did Dupin know the minister in question well or only slightly? 2. Was the minister a timid or a daring man? 3. Was the minister

familiar or unfamiliar with the usual methods of the police? 4. Was the minister therefore prepared or unprepared against such methods? 5. Was the minister seldom absent from home at night or was he frequently absent? 6. Were these absences, in Dupin's opinion, accidental or on purpose? 7. If the absences were planned, what was their purpose? 8. Did the minister succeed or fail in his efforts to deceive the police? 9. Do you think the police acted wisely or stupidly in this affair? 10. Are police methods, in your opinion, generally clever or stupid? 11. What was Dupin's purpose in wearing black glasses when he went to visit the minister? 12. Why do people normally wear black glasses? 13. Are black glasses used more often in the winter or in the summer? 14. Was it a large box or a small box which Dupin noticed on the mantelpiece? 15. What was in the box? 16. Was the letter in the box the same in appearance as the original letter or had it been altered? 17. What personal article did Dupin leave intentionally in the minister's apartment? 18. On Dupin's second visit what sudden noise was heard in the street? 19. What did Dupin do while the minister rushed to the window? 20. Why did Dupin think it wise to leave an exact copy of the letter in the box on the mantelpiece?

B. Vocabulary Drill. Choose The Correct Form:

1. The person *in question* is the person (whom I wish to question, whom we have been discussing, about whom I wish to ask some questions).

2. A synonym for *permit* is (refuse, allow, dare, enjoy).

3. Give the opposites of these words: weak, dark, small, full, dirty, simple, carelessly, feminine, first, alive.

4. To *call upon someone* is to (criticize him, admire him, telephone him, visit him).

5. Give the corresponding noun form of these adjectives: suspicious, different, clever, dangerous, foolish.

6. In what two different ways can the following word be pronounced: *tear?* What different meanings does the word have when pronounced in these two ways?

7. Distinguish in meaning between *inside out* and *upside down?*

8. To *converse* with someone is to (visit him, listen to him, talk with him, call him up).

9. Which of these past tense forms are pronounced as words of one syllable and which are pronounced as words of two syllables: stepped, looked, changed, forced, needed, placed, wanted?

10. A common synonym for *pistol* is (revolver, rifle, cannon, shot).

C. Use These In Sentences:

in question, to be familiar with, as a result of, to prevent from doing, to put on, to be able to, as soon as, to look for, to call upon, in order to.

THE LAST LEAF

O. Henry

PART I

To Greenwich Village, which is a section of New York City, many people came who were interested in art. They liked the bohemian life of the village, and they enjoyed living among so many artists. The buildings and apartments were often very old and dirty, but this only added to the interest of the place.

At the top of an old three-story brick house Sue and Johnsy had their studio. One of them was from the state of Maine, the other from California. They had met in the restaurant of an Eighth Street hotel. Both were artists who had recently come to New York to make their living.

That was in May. In November, a cold, unseen stranger,

whom the doctors called pneumonia, visited the city, touching one here and one there with his icy finger.

He touched Johnsy and she lay, scarcely moving, on her painted iron bed, looking through the small window at the blank wall of the opposite building.

One morning the busy doctor invited Sue into the hall.

"She has about one chance in ten to live," he said as he shook down the mercury in his clinical thermometer. "And that one chance depends upon her desire to get better. But your little friend has made up her mind that she is going to die. Is she worrying about something?"

"She wanted to paint a picture of the Bay of Naples some day," said Sue.

"No, something more important — a man perhaps?"

"No."

"Well, perhaps it is a result of her fever and her general physical weakness. But when a patient begins to feel sure that she is going to die, then I subtract fifty per cent from the power of medicines. If you can succeed in making her interested in something, in asking, for instance, about the latest styles in women's clothes, then I can promise you a one-to-five chance for her instead of one-to-ten."

After the doctor had gone, Sue went into her own room and cried. Later, trying not to show her sadness, she went into Johnsy's room, whistling.

Johnsy lay under the bedclothes, with her face toward the window. Sue stopped whistling, thinking Johnsy was asleep. But soon Sue heard a low sound, several times repeated. Sue went quickly to the bedside.

Johnsy's eyes were wide open. She was looking out of the window, and counting backwards.

"Twelve," she said, and a little later, "eleven," and then "ten" and "nine" and then "eight" — "seven."

PART II

Sue looked out of the window. What was Johnsy counting? There was only a gray, back yard and the blank wall of the opposite house. An old, old vine, dead at the roots, climbed halfway up the wall. The cold breath of autumn had blown almost all the leaves from the vine until its branches were almost bare.

"What is it, dear?" asked Sue.

"Six," said Johnsy very quietly. "They are falling faster now. Three days ago there were almost a hundred. It makes my head ache to count them. But now it's easy. There goes another one. There are only five left now."

"Five what, dear? Tell me!" said Sue.

"Leaves. The leaves of that vine. When the last leaf of that vine falls, I must go too. I've known that for three days. Didn't the doctor tell you?"

"The doctor didn't say any such thing. That is pure foolishness," said Sue. "What connection have those old leaves with your getting well? And you used to love that old vine so much. Please don't be silly. The doctor told me this morning that your chances of getting well soon were excellent. Now try to take some of your soup and let me get back to work so that I can make money to buy you some good port wine."

"There's no use buying any more wine," said Johnsy, keeping her eyes fixed on the blank wall of the house opposite. "There goes another leaf. That leaves just four. I want to see the last one fall before it gets dark. Then I'll go too."

"Johnsy, dear," said Sue, bending over her, "will you promise me to keep your eyes closed and not look out of the window until I have finished working? I must deliver these drawings tomorrow. I need the light; otherwise I would pull down the curtain."

"Can't you draw in your room?" said Johnsy coldly.

"I'd rather stay here with you," said Sue. "Besides, I don't want you to keep looking at those silly leaves."

"Tell me as soon as you have finished," said Johnsy, closing her eyes and lying white and still. "Because I want to see the last leaf fall. I'm tired of waiting. I'm tired of thinking."

"Try to sleep," said Sue a little later. "I must go downstairs for a minute to get Mr. Behrman who is going to sit as my model. But I will be right back. And don't move and also please promise me not to look out of the window."

Old Mr. Behrman was a painter who lived on the first floor beneath them. He was more than sixty years old. Behrman was a failure in art. He had always wanted to paint a masterpiece, but he had never yet begun to paint it. For many years he had painted nothing, except now and then something in the line of commercial or advertising work. He earned a little money by serving as a model for those young artists who could not pay the price for a regular model. He drank much whiskey and when he was drunk always talked about the great masterpiece he was going to paint. He was a fierce, intense little man who considered himself as a watch-dog and protector for the two young artists living above him, of whom he was very fond.

PART III

Sue found Behrman in his poorly-lighted studio. In one corner of the room stood a blank canvas which had been waiting for twenty-five years to receive the first line of the promised masterpiece. Sue told him of the strange idea which Johnsy had concerning the last leaf, and said that she feared that Johnsy would really die when the last leaf fell.

Old Behrman shouted, "Are there people in the world who are foolish enough to die simply because leaves fall from an old vine? I have never heard of such a thing. Why do you permit such silly ideas to come into her mind? Oh, that poor little Miss Johnsy."

"She is very ill and very weak," explained Sue, "and the fever has left her mind full of strange ideas."

Johnsy was sleeping when they both went upstairs. Sue pulled down the curtain and motioned to Behrman to go into the other room. There they looked out of the window fearfully at the vine. Then they looked at each other for a moment without speaking. A cold rain was falling, mixed with snow. Behrman took a seat and prepared himself to pose for Sue as a model.

When Sue woke up the next morning, she found Johnsy with dull, wide open eyes, looking at the window.

"Put up the curtain. I want to see," Johnsy said quietly.

Sue obeyed.

But, oh, after the heavy rain and the strong wind, one leaf was still hanging on the vine. The last leaf. Still dark green, it hung from a branch some twenty feet above the ground.

"It is the last one," said Johnsy. "I thought it would surely fall during the night. I heard the wind and the rain. It will fall today and I shall die at the same time."

"Dear Johnsy," said Sue, placing her face close to Johnsy's on the pillow, "think of me if you won't think of yourself. What shall I do?"

The day passed slowly, and even through the growing darkness of the evening they could see the lone leaf still hanging from the branch against the wall. And then, with the coming of the night, the wind began to blow again, and the rain began to fall heavily.

But the next morning when Johnsy commanded that the curtain be raised again, the leaf was still there.

Johnsy lay for a long time looking at it. And then she called to Sue.

"I've been a bad girl, Sue," said Johnsy. "Something has

made the last leaf stay there just to show me how bad I was. It was a sin to want to die. You may bring me a little soup now — and then put some pillows behind me and I will sit up and watch you cook."

An hour later Johnsy said, "Sue, some day I want to paint a picture of the Bay of Naples."

The doctor came in the afternoon. "You are doing fine," he said, taking Johnsy's thin hand in his. "In another week or so you will be perfectly well. And now I must go to see another patient downstairs. His name is Behrman. He is some kind of artist, I believe. Pneumonia, too. He is an old, weak man, and the attack is very severe. There is no hope for him, but I am sending him to the hospital in order to make him more comfortable."

The next day, Sue came to the bed where Johnsy lay. "The doctor tells me that soon you will be perfectly well again," Sue said, putting her arm around Johnsy. Johnsy smiled at her happily.

"Isn't it wonderful?" Sue continued. "But now I have something important to tell you. Old Mr. Behrman died in the hospital this morning of pneumonia. He was sick only two days. They found him in his room the morning of the first day helpless with pain and fever. His shoes and clothing were completely wet and icy cold. They couldn't figure out where he had been on such a terrible night. And then they found a lantern, still lighted, a ladder, and some other things which showed that, during the wind and the rain, he had climbed up and painted a green leaf on the wall of the house opposite. Didn't you think it was strange that the leaf never moved when the wind blew? Ah, darling, it was Behrman's real masterpiece, — he painted it there the night that the last leaf fell."

Exercises Based on

THE LAST LEAF

PART I

A. Answer These Questions:

1. In what section of New York City does this story take place? 2. What other sections of New York City have you heard of? 3. For what is Greenwich Village famous? 4. Is Greenwich Village one of the older or newer sections of New York City? 5. Is this story concerned with two young artists or two young engineers? 6. Had these young artists been born in New York City or had they come to New York to make their living? 7. Where were you born? 8. Of what disease was there an epidemic at this time? 9. Is pneumonia a serious disease or an unimportant disease? 10. Is pneumonia more serious or less serious than influenza? 11. What is the present medical treatment for pneumonia? 12. Did both of the young artists of this story fall ill or only one of them? 13. Was Johnsy seriously ill or only slightly ill? 14. Have you ever been seriously ill? 15. When were you last ill and what illness did you have? 16. Did the doctor think that Johnsy's chances of recovery were good or bad? 17. Did Johnsy have a strong desire to get well or was she indifferent to her condition? 18. Did Sue laugh or cry when she heard the doctor's report on her friend's condition? 19. Did she show her sadness when she went into Johnsy's room or did she try to hide it by whistling? 20. Was Johnsy lying with her face toward the window or away from the window when Sue entered?

B. Vocabulary Drill. Choose The Correct Form:

1. Greenwich Village is a section in which of these cities (Chicago, Paris, New York, Boston).

2. Artists usually work in a room which they call their (office, studio, closet, hall).

3. Cross out the silent letters in these words: pneumonia, thumb, honest, Christmas, half, walk, would, whistle, climb.

4. Something which is *icy* is (very hot, very cold, sticky, worn out).

5. A synonym for *scarcely* is (often, hurriedly, curiously, hardly).

6. *To make up one's mind* means to (hesitate, think something over, decide, refuse).

7. Give the opposites of these words: backwards, to succeed, to stop, asleep, quickly, low, later, important, better, dirty, old, to add, top.

8. Give the corresponding noun form of these adjectives: weak, sad, wide, important, dirty, icy.

9. Which of these metals is often used in making thermometers (iron, silver, lead, mercury)?

10. Give the past tense form and the past participial form of these verbs: shake, come, add, meet, lie, die, make, have, begin, feel, go.

C. Use These In Sentences:

to be interested in, to make one's living, at the top (bottom), to make up one's mind, to worry about, to feel sure, to succeed in, for instance, wide open, to look out of.

PART II

A. Answer These Questions:

1. What was the sick girl counting as she looked out of the window? 2. Did these leaves grow on a tree or on a vine? 3. Which is larger, a tree or a vine? 4. How high do vines sometimes grow? 5. Were there many leaves or few leaves on the vine when Sue began to count them? 6. What was causing the leaves to fall so rapidly? 7. Was the weather cold or warm at this time? 8. In what season of the year do leaves appear on trees and vines and in what season do they fall? 9. What did Johnsy think would happen when the last leaf fell? 10. Was there any reason for her having such a fantastic idea? 11. Who was old Behrman? 12. Did he live on the floor beneath the girls or on the floor above them? 13. Was Behrman a young man or an old man? 14. Had Behrman been a success in art or a failure? 15. Did he drink much whiskey or little whiskey? 16. Had he ever painted a

great masterpiece or did he only talk about painting a masterpiece? 17. What is a masterpiece? 18. What masterpieces of literature have you read in English? 19. What masterpieces of painting have you seen or heard of? 20. Did Behrman hire models to sit for him or did he serve as a model for those artists who could not afford to pay regular models?

B. Vocabulary Drill. Choose The Correct Form:

1. *Silly* means (seldom, sad, weak, foolish).
2. The word *climb* is pronounced to rhyme with (limb, dumb, damn, time).
3. Which one of these words is not spelled correctly: excelent, connection, climbed, commercial, masterpiece?
4. Give the plurals of these words: leaf, chance, key, city, watch, wish, knife, box.
5. *Besides* means (alongside of, near, in addition, seldom).
6. Distinguish in meaning between *besides* and *beside.*
7. The word *ache* is pronounced to rhyme with (catch, touch, like, take).
8. The opposite of *drunk* is (sane, sick, sour, sober).
9. Give the corresponding noun form of these verbs: fail, serve, consider, deliver, breathe, connect, protect.
10. *I'd rather stay* means that I (must stay, ought to stay, insist on staying, prefer to stay).

C. Use These In Sentences:

to make one's head ache, to be left, to get back, to make money, to bend over, to pull down, I'd rather . . ., to be tired of, to be right back.

PART III

A. Answer These Questions:

1. How many leaves remained on the vine the following morning? 2. What had happened to the remaining leaves? 3. Had the wind been strong or weak during the night? 4. Did the last leaf fall during the day or did it remain on the vine? 5. Did Johnsy now begin to feel better or worse? 6. Did she begin to eat again or did she cease to

eat? 7. Did her interest in her painting revive or disappear? 8. Of what famous Bay did she wish to paint a picture? 9. Where is the Bay of Naples located? 10. Was the doctor pleased or displeased with the change in Johnsy's condition? 11. What other patient did the doctor have to go to see? 12. From what illness was this patient suffering? 13. Did the doctor say that the attack was light or severe? 14. Did the doctor say that there was much hope or no hope for Behrman's recovery? 15. What finally happened to Behrman in the hospital? 16. Was his illness of short duration or of long duration? 17. In what way had Behrman become sick? 18. What had he painted on the wall opposite Johnsy's room? 19. Had the weather been pleasant or unpleasant the night when he painted his last masterpiece? 20. Was Behrman's last act a selfish or a generous one?

B. Vocabulary Drill. Choose The Correct Form:

1. To *fear* something is to (be afraid of it, enjoy it, respect it, look it over).

2. *Canvas* is a (large fish, kind of heavy cloth, blank paper, kind of paint).

3. A common synonym for *ill* is (weak, healthy, dishonest, sick).

4. We usually find *pillows* on a (dressing table, chest of drawers, bed, night table).

5. If I say that I can't *figure something out*, I mean that I can't (carry it, afford it, understand it).

6. Which of these will light your way at night (a masterpiece, a lantern, a watch-dog, a good doctor)?

7. Which of these can you use to climb the side of a building (a ladder, a branch, an epidemic, a dying vine)?

8. What two different meanings does the word *lie* have?

9. The word *passed* is pronounced to rhyme with (least, fast, lasted, insist).

10. Which of these past tense forms are pronounced as words of one syllable and which are pronounced as words of two syllables: feared, pulled, died, looked, wanted, passed, raised, called, counted, smiled, lighted, climbed, painted, moved?

MR. TRAVERS' FIRST HUNT

Richard Harding Davis

PART I

Young Travers, who was going to marry a girl on Long Island, met her father and brother only a few days before the wedding. The father and brother were both very much interested in horses. They owned many fine horses and they liked nothing better than to talk about horses all day long and every evening. Old Paddock, the father, had often said that, when a young man asked for his permission to marry his daughter, he would ask the young man in return, not if he lived straight, but if he could ride straight. And if the young man answered *yes* to this question, then he would receive the father's permission to marry the girl.

Travers had met Miss Paddock and her mother while traveling in Europe. Thus he did not meet the father and brother until he was invited to their home just a few days before the wedding. Unfortunately, this happened during the hunting season. He spent the early part of the first evening talking alone with Miss Paddock in a corner of the room, but later, when the women had gone to bed, the father and son approached him. Young Paddock said, "You ride, of course, Mr. Travers." Now Mr. Travers had never ridden a horse in his entire life, and he was, in fact, very much afraid of horses; but Miss Paddock had told him earlier that he must answer *yes* to this question. Therefore, Travers said that there was nothing he liked better than to ride horses. In fact, he said that he would rather ride than eat or sleep.

"That's fine," said young Paddock. "In that case I'll give you our horse, Satan, for the hunt tomorrow morning. Satan is always a little difficult to control at the beginning of the season, and last year he killed one of our workmen. Since that time none of us like to ride him. But you can probably control him easily."

Mr. Travers did not sleep very well that night and dreamed of taking long jumps into space on a wild horse that breathed fire from its nose.

The next morning he wanted to say that he was ill — and, in fact, he did not feel too well. But he knew that he would probably have to ride a horse sometime during his visit, so he decided to do his best. The weather was rather bad, and the sky was dark. Travers hoped that perhaps the hunt would be cancelled. But, as he lay in doubt, the servant knocked at the door with his riding clothes and his hot water.

He came downstairs looking very sad. Satan had been taken to the place where all the hunters were supposed to meet. Travers felt very weak in his stomach when he saw Satan because the horse was pulling three of the servants, who were trying to hold him, off their feet. Travers decided that he would wait until the other hunters had left before he got on the horse, so that no one could see what a poor rider he was. Thus, when all the dogs had left and the hunters had started off at a gallop after the dogs, Travers closed his teeth tightly, pulled his hat down over his ears, and climbed up into the saddle. His feet fell, by accident, into the right position, and the next instant he started off, with the feeling that he was riding on top of a fast locomotive.

PART II

Satan had passed all the other horses in less than five minutes and was soon close to the dogs who were by this time following the fox. It was impossible for Travers to hold the horse back. Travers had taken hold of the horse's saddle with both hands, and he held on with all his strength. He shut his eyes whenever Satan jumped, and he never knew how he happened to remain in the saddle. Fortunately, he was so far ahead of the other riders that no one was able to see how badly he rode. In any case, he led all the other hunters in bravery and speed, and not even Young Paddock was near him from the very beginning of the hunt.

There was a broad hill in front of him and another hill just on the other side of the first hill. There was also a broad stream between the two hills. No one had ever tried to jump over this stream on a horse. It was considered more of a swim than anything else, and the hunters always crossed it by a bridge to the left. Travers saw the bridge and tried to pull Satan's head in that direction, but Satan kept straight on like an express train. They went down the first hill toward the stream as if they were traveling on level land. The hunters in the rear gave a cry of warning but Travers only closed his eyes and held on to the saddle tightly. He remembered that Satan had killed one man previously, and he trembled. Then Satan suddenly rose in the air so high that Travers thought they would never come down again, but the horse did come down again safely on the other side of the stream. Travers, by some magic, still remained in the saddle. The next minute Satan was over the second hill and had stopped in the very center of the dogs who by now had finally captured the fox which they had been following. And then Travers showed that he was a specialist in riding horses even though, really he could not ride at all, for he took out his cigar case, and when the other hunters came up over the bridge and around the hill they saw Travers seated comfortably on his horse. He was calmly smoking a cigar and patting Satan affectionately on the head.

"My dear girl," said old Mr. Paddock to his daughter that evening after the hunt, "if you love that young man and want to keep him alive, make him promise to give up riding horses. I have never seen a better or a braver horseman. Today he took several very dangerous jumps. But some day he is going to break his neck, and he should be stopped."

Young Paddock, in turn, was so well pleased by his future brother-in-law's excellent riding ability that, in the smoking room that evening before all the men, he offered to give him Satan as a present.

"No," said Travers sadly. "I can't accept. Your sister has already asked me to give up what is more important to me than anything else in life, and that is my riding. You see, she is worried about my safety and has asked me to promise her that I will never ride again. Therefore I have given her my word."

All the men protested loudly.

"Yes, I know," said Travers to young Paddock. "It is difficult, but it shows what sacrifices a man will make for the woman he loves."

Exercises Based on

MR. TRAVERS' FIRST HUNT

PART I

A. Answer These Questions:

1. In what kind of animal were the father and brother of Miss Paddock greatly interested? 2. Did they own many or few horses? 3. Is the horse a wild animal or a domestic animal? 4. Is it easy or difficult to learn to ride a horse? 5. Was young Travers able or unable to ride a horse? 6. Had he had much or little experience in riding? 7. Did he look forward with great pleasure or with little pleasure to the next morning's ride? 8. Why did Travers tell the father and brother of Miss Paddock that he rode well? 9. What kind of horse did they promise to give Travers for the hunt the next day? 10. What had the horse "Satan" done to one of the workmen the previous year? 11. Was Satan easy or difficult to control? 12. Did this story take place during the hunting season or during the fishing season? 13. What season of the year is the best season for hunting? 14. Did Travers sleep well or badly that night? 15. Do you usually sleep well or badly? 16. How many hours a night do you usually sleep? 17. Did Travers look happy or sad as he came downstairs the next morning? 18. Why did Travers wait until the other riders had left before he got on the horse? 19. Was he successful or unsuccessful in getting on the horse? 20. Did the horse start off slowly or rapidly?

B. Vocabulary Drill. Choose The Correct Form:

1. He would *rather ride* means that he (often rides, preferred to ride, seldom rode, hoped to ride).

2. The contraction *I'll* is pronounced to rhyme with (hill, mail, mile, feel).

3. Which one of these words is not spelled correctly: difficult, beginning, gallop, probably, locomotive, supposed?

4. To *cancel* something is to (put it away, look it up, look it over, call it off).

5. In which of these words is the letter *s* pronounced like *s* and in which is it pronounced like *z*: nose, case, dogs, ears, hats, us, is, days, was, as, easy, best?

6. Give the opposites of these words: tight, off, top, fast, long, wild, difficult, ill, best.

7. *Rather late* means (very late, somewhat late, a little late, not very late).

8. Give the corresponding adverb form of these adjectives: easy, happy, hard, good, bad, tight, fast.

9. Use each of these words in a sentence, once as a noun and once as a verb: hand, place, start, ride, hunt, dream, jump, answer, question.

10. Give the corresponding noun form of these verbs: marry, breathe, permit, invite, remain, begin, decide.

C. Use These In Sentences:

to be interested in, all day long, to ask for, to go to bed, to ride a horse, would rather ride, to dream of, to do one's best, to be supposed to.

PART II

A. Answer These Questions:

1. Did Satan run slowly or swiftly? 2. Did he pass all the other horses or did he remain far behind? 3. Was he soon close to the dogs or far behind them? 4. What animal were the dogs following? 5. Was it possible or impossible for Travers to hold the horse back? 6. Did he take hold of the saddle with only one hand or with both hands? 7. Did he shut his eyes or open his eyes whenever Satan jumped? 8. Did Satan jump across the broad stream ahead or did he cross it by the bridge at the left? 9. Was this an easy jump or an extremely dangerous one? 10. What advice did old Mr. Paddock give Miss Paddock that evening regarding Travers? 11. Did he consider Travers a daring or a timid rider? 12. Was young Paddock pleased or displeased with Travers' riding ability? 13. What present did he offer Travers that evening in the smoking room? 14. Did Travers accept or refuse Young Paddock's offer? 15. Did the other men approve or protest Travers' refusal to accept Satan? 16. What explanation did

Travers give for refusing young Paddock's offer? 17. Did Travers claim that it was easy or difficult for him to give up riding horses? 18. For whom did he say he was making this great sacrifice? 19. Was it really a great sacrifice for him or not? 20. Was Travers thus successful or unsuccessful in winning the hand of the woman whom he loved?

B. Vocabulary Drill. Choose The Correct Form:

1. A common synonym for *broad* is (long, short, narrow, wide).
2. In what two different ways may the word *close* be pronounced? What different meaning does the word have when pronounced in these two different ways?
3. The opposite of to *take hold of* is to (hold on to, pull back, let go of, throw away).
4. A *saddle* is generally made of (wood, cloth, plastic, leather).
5. Give the corresponding noun form of these adjectives: strong, fortunate, brave, safe, possible, comfortable, affectionate, dangerous, important, difficult.
6. Give the past tense form and the past participial form of these verbs: rise, step, lead, pass, swim, ride, take, see, keep, give, show. Which of these verbs are "regular" in form and which are "irregular"?
7. Which of these verbs have the same form in the past tense as in the present tense: cut, take, shut, put, close, hit, hate, read?
8. To *give one's word* is to (hesitate, promise, refuse, deny).
9. How many syllables does each of these words contain and on which syllable does the accent fall: excellent, jumped, promised, therefore, comfortably, passed, affectionate, ability?
10. A common synonym for *fortunate* is (early, lucky, late, famous).

C. Use These In Sentences:

to take hold of, to hold on, in front of, to keep straight on, in the very center, at all, to take out, to give up, to be worried about.

THE HUNGRY MAN WAS FED

Richard Harding Davis

PART I

Mr. Van Bibber broke one of the rules of his life one day, left his private club, and went downtown. This unusual event occurred as a result of a call by his lawyer, who wished to have Van Bibber's signature on some important letters and documents. It had been five years since Van Bibber had come so far downtown. As he walked through the busy streets, he looked about him at the many new business buildings, shops, and stores. He was as confused as a newly arrived immigrant by the great activity which he met on every side.

At first he rather enjoyed the novelty of the situation, and after he had completed his business at the lawyer's office he tried to walk along lower Broadway in the same calm, quiet way that he walked along Fifth Avenue, where his aristocratic and elegant club was situated.

But everybody seemed to be very busy and in a great hurry. People struck against him, and when he crossed the streets the automobiles tried to strike him down. He recognized a few people whom he knew fairly well, but they were all in such a hurry and they seemed to be so surprised at seeing him that Van Bibber began to feel very uncomfortable. And so he decided to go back to his usual seat in his club window uptown as soon as possible.

"Hello, Van Bibber," said one of the young men who was passing. "What brings you down here? Have you lost your way?"

"I think I have," said Van Bibber. "If you'll kindly tell me how I can get back to civilization again, I shall be very grateful."

"Take the subway from Park Place," said his friend from over his shoulder as he disappeared suddenly into the crowd.

Van Bibber had no very clear idea as to where Park Place was. But he walked along Broadway a little distance and then turned into another street. Presently, a poor, dirty, and red-eyed man approached him and asked Van Bibber for a few cents to buy food. "I've come all the way from Chicago," said the man. "And I haven't had any food for twenty-four hours."

Van Bibber drew back as though the man had a serious disease and handed him a quarter without waiting to receive the man's thanks.

"Poor fellow," said Van Bibber. "Imagine going without dinner all day." Van Bibber could not imagine this even though he tried, and the idea of going without dinner seemed to be such an impossible one that he decided to go back and find the man and give him more money. Van Bibber's ideas of dinner were rather special. He did not know that there were restaurants where one could get a good meal for a quarter, including roast beef, vegetables, and dessert. He hardly considered a quarter sufficient tip for the waiter who served him his dinner and certainly not for the dinner itself. Van Bibber did not see the man at first, and when he finally found him the man did not see him. Van Bibber stood for a minute watching the man and while he watched him he saw him stop three other gentlemen, each of whom gave him some money. Then the man approached Van Bibber again, repeated his sad story, and asked him for money again. He evidently did not recognize Van Bibber, and the latter gave him a half-dollar and walked away feeling that the man must certainly have enough money by this time with which to get something to eat, if only lunch.

PART II

In returning to find this man, Van Bibber had become a little confused in his directions, and he went completely around the block before he discovered he had lost his way. He was now standing exactly where he had started. Suddenly the same man approached him again and gave him the same familiar story. He had just come from Chicago, he had not eaten in twenty-four hours, etc.

This time the man looked a little uneasy. He was not sure whether he had approached this particular gentleman before. But Van Bibber had a clever idea and put his hand quickly into his pocket as if he were about to give him some money.

"Nothing to eat for twenty-four hours!" said Van Bibber. "And you haven't any money either?"

"Not a cent," said the man sadly. "And I'm weak from lack of food. I hate to ask for money, it's not the money I want. It's just the food. I'm dying from hunger."

"Well," said Van Bibber suddenly, "if it is only something

to eat which you want, come in here with me and I will buy you your breakfast." But the man held back and insisted that they would not permit a man like him to enter such a fine restaurant.

"Oh, yes, they will," said Van Bibber, looking at the menu placed in the window of the place. "It seems to me to be extremely cheap. Go on in!" he added, and there was something in his tone of voice which made the man enter quickly into the eating place.

It was a strange place, Van Bibber thought, and the people looked curiously at his elegant dress, his manners, his gloves, the flower in the buttonhole of his coat. They also looked curiously at the miserably dressed object who accompanied him.

"You aren't going to eat two breakfasts, are you?" asked one of the waiters, addressing himself to Van Bibber's companion. The latter looked a little uneasy, and Van Bibber, in turn, smiled quietly in triumph.

"You are mistaken," Van Bibber said to the waiter. "This man is starving. He has not tasted food for twenty-four hours. Give him whatever he asks for."

Van Bibber's companion looked very unhappy. The waiter smiled and winked at Van Bibber. The man ordered milk, but Van Bibber protested and ordered two beefsteaks and fried potatoes, hot rolls, two eggs, coffee, and ham and bacon.

"Heavens! What do you think I am?" cried the man.

"Hungry," said Van Bibber, very softly. "Or are you an impostor? And, you know, if you are an impostor, I shall have to hand you over to the police."

Van Bibber now seemed to be enjoying himself very much. There was a policeman standing across the street, and occasionally Van Bibber would look at his companion and then point toward the policeman. His companion had begun to eat the meal which the waiter had brought him, but was not enjoying it at all. He kept cursing loudly as he ate.

PART III

Whenever the man stopped eating, Van Bibber would point to a still unfinished dish, and the man, after strong protest, would attack it again as if it were poison. The people who were sitting nearby were laughing, and the proprietor behind the desk was smiling.

"There," said the man at last. "I've eaten all I can eat for a year. You think you are very clever, don't you? But if you want to spend your money so foolishly, that's your business. Only don't let me catch you around these streets at night, that's all."

And the man started to leave, shaking his fist at Van Bibber.

"Wait a minute," said Van Bibber. "You haven't paid them for your breakfast."

"Haven't what?" cried the man. "Paid them? How could I pay them? You invited me in here to eat. I didn't want any breakfast, did I? You'll have to pay for your fun yourself, or they will throw you out. Don't try to be too clever."

"I gave you seventy-five cents with which to buy breakfast. This check calls for eighty-five cents, and it is very cheap," said Van Bibber, bowing politely toward the proprietor. "Several other gentlemen also gave you money for breakfast when you told them that you were starving. You have the money with you now. So pay what you owe at once, or I'll call that police officer," he said.

The man started to run toward the door, but the waiter ran after him, took hold of him by the neck and held him.

"Let me go," cried the man. "Let me go and I'll pay you."

Everybody in the restaurant came up now and formed a

circle around the group and watched the man count out eighty-five cents into the waiter's hand, which left him just ten cents to himself.

"You have forgotten to tip the waiter who served you," said Van Bibber, smiling and pointing at the ten cent piece which remained.

"No," said the man strongly.

"Oh, yes," said Van Bibber, "Do the right thing now or I'll . . ."

Then the man dropped the ten cent piece into the waiter's hand, and Van Bibber, smiling, made his way through the admiring crowd and out into the street.

"I suspect," said Van Bibber later in the day when re-telling his adventure to a friend, "that after I left, the fellow tried to get that tip back from the waiter, for I saw him come out of the place very suddenly, and without touching the pavement he landed on his back in the street. That waiter was certainly a powerful fellow."

Exercises Based on

THE HUNGRY MAN WAS FED

PART I

A. Answer These Questions:

1. Did Van Bibber go downtown as a result of a call by his lawyer or by his doctor? 2. Did he often go downtown or had it been many years since he had been downtown? 3. Did Van Bibber live in an apartment or in a private club? 4. What kind of people usually live in private clubs? 5. Do you imagine Van Bibber to have been a poor man or a rich man? 6. Do you imagine him to have been a fat man

or a thin man; a young man or an elderly man? 7. Why was Van Bibber somewhat confused by the great activity of the downtown streets? 8. Did he begin to feel comfortable or uncomfortable in the middle of all this activity? 9. To what means of transportation did his friend direct him? 10. What different means of transportation are there in New York? 11. Do the subways go under the surface or above the surface of the ground? 12. Are there subways in all important cities or only in a few very important cities? 13. Is the subway faster or slower than the bus? 14. Which do you consider more convenient, the bus or the subway? 15. Who finally approached Van Bibber on the street and begged money for food? 16. What story did the man tell Van Bibber? 17. How much money did Van Bibber give the man? 18. Why did Van Bibber go back a second time to give the man more money? 19. When Van Bibber returned, what did he see the man doing? 20. Did the man recognize Van Bibber or did he foolishly repeat his story and ask him again for money?

B. Vocabulary Drill. Choose The Correct Form:

1. A common synonym for *occurred* is (arrived, delayed, happened, walked).

2. Distinguish in meaning between the two words *immigrant* and *emigrant.*

3. A common synonym for *situated* is (needed, lost, decided, located).

4. The word *crossed* is pronounced to rhyme with (toast, lost, used, wrist).

5. *Fairly well* means (very well, not at all well, pretty well, well enough).

6. A synonym for *grateful* is (funny, agreeable, thankful, disappointed).

7. *Presently* means (at this moment, very soon, some time ago, a little while ago).

8. A synonym for *evidently* is (always, probably, apparently, seldom).

9. In a restaurant, after a meal, it is customary to give the waiter a (note of thanks, dirty look, tip, few pennies).

10. Give the corresponding noun form af these adjectives: active, elegant, sad, dirty, serious, comfortable, possible, kind.

C. Use These In Sentences:

as a result of, in a hurry, as soon as possible, to lose one's way, all the way, to draw back, to ask for, at first, by this time.

PART II

A. Answer These Questions:

1. How many times in all did the man approach Van Bibber and ask for money? 2. Did he tell the same story each time or a different story? 3. What was the story which he told each time? 4. Did he say he had just eaten or that he had not eaten for twenty-four hours? 5. Did the man say that he was dying of hunger or of thirst? 6. What did Van Bibber finally want the man to do? 7. Why did the man not wish to go into the restaurant with Van Bibber? 8. What excuse did he give Van Bibber for not wishing to go into the restaurant? 9. Was the restaurant a cheap restaurant or an expensive restaurant? 10. Is the food generally better in a cheap restaurant or in an expensive restaurant? 11. In which type of restaurant is the service generally better? 12. What is the difference between a restaurant and a cafeteria? 13. Which are generally cheaper, restaurants or cafeterias? 14. Did the man at first order a large breakfast or a small breakfast? 15. What additional food did Van Bibber then order for the man? 16. Do you usually eat a large breakfast or a small breakfast? 18. In your native country, what do the people generally eat for breakfast? 19. What did Van Bibber threaten to do if the man did not eat his food? 20. Why did the man keep cursing loudly as he ate?

B. Vocabulary Drill. Choose The Correct Form:

1. A common, colloquial synonym for *confused* is (uneasy, difficult, mixed up, worn out).

2. Which of these do we find only in a restaurant (time-table, deposit-slip, menu, price tag)?

3. *Extremely cheap* means (rather cheap, very expensive, not at all cheap, very cheap).

4. The opposite of *latter* is (sooner, earlier, former, brighter).

5. Give the opposites of these words by adding to each one the necessary prefix: happy, easy, possible, definite, honest, kind, experienced.

6. A person *winks*, using his (eye, ear, nose, throat).

7. A common, colloquial synonym for *occasionally* is (often, every other day, now and then, seldom).

8. To *starve* is to (make good time, die of hunger, suffer from thirst, be satisfied).

9. A common synonym for *mistaken* is (mixed up, right, out of step, wrong).

10. Express these in negative form: he saw, he drew back, he took, I think, he said, I have, I've had, he broke, it had been.

C. Use These In Sentences:

to become confused, around the block, to be weak from, to die from, to hold back, to be mistaken, in turn, to hand over, to point toward.

PART III

A. Answer These Questions:

1. Were the other diners in the restaurant amused or annoyed at Van Bibber's action? 2. Was the proprietor behind the desk amused or annoyed? 3. What is the difference between the proprietor of a restaurant and the manager? 4. Did the man intend to pay for the breakfast himself or did he expect Van Bibber to pay for it? 5. Was it necessary or unnecessary for Van Bibber to call the police officer? 6. Was the police officer in the restaurant or was he standing across the street? 7. What, in general, are some of the duties of a police officer? 8. To what extent is the work of a police officer dangerous? 9. Who finally paid for the meal? 10. Who also had to leave a tip for the waiter? 11. What, in general, is the purpose of tipping? 12. Do you in general approve or disapprove of the custom of tipping? 13. How much did the man tip the waiter? 14. Who smiled when the man tipped the waiter, Van Bibber or the man? 15. Was the waiter a slight or a powerfully built fellow? 16. When the man started to run toward the door, what did the waiter do? 17. Did the breakfast cost more or less than the money Van Bibber gave the man? 18. What was Van Bibber's reply to the man's statement that Van

Bibber should pay for the meal? 19. Was Van Bibber foolish or clever in taking the man in to breakfast? 20. Did Van Bibber keep his adventure a secret or did he tell it to his friends?

B. Vocabulary Drill. Choose The Correct Form:

1. The word *laugh* is pronounced to rhyme with (ought, rough, half, saw).
2. What two different meanings can the word *still* have?
3. A common synonym for *proprietor* is (waiter, customer, owner, tenant).
4. What two different meanings and pronunciations can the word *bow* have?
5. The word *owe* is pronounced to rhyme with (sew, new, two, saw).
6. Change these phrases to interrogative (question) form: he dropped it, he did it, you have forgotten, you paid him, he ran after him, he'll call us.
7. Pick out the silent letters in each of these words: knife, laugh, attack, climb, wrong, honest, half, knew.
8. Use each of these words in sentences, once as a noun and once as a verb: land, point, paint, smile, place, start, protest, attack, cry.
9. Which one of these words is not spelled correctly: nearby, gentelman, restaurant, powerful, circle, synonym?
10. How many syllables does each of these words contain and on which syllable does the accent fall: remained, waiter's, foolishly, toward, dropped, looked, certainly, adventure, proprietor?

C. Use These In Sentences:

to point to (at), as if, to pay for, to throw someone out, at once, to run after, to take hold of, to count out, to make one's way through something.

DAVID SWAN

Nathaniel Hawthorne

PART I

We know very little about the early events which influence our course through life. Some of these events — if such they can be called — come very close to us but pass us by without apparent result and often without any indication of their coming or going. If we knew all the possible changes in our fortune, life would be too full of hopes and fears, of surprises and disappointments, to permit us a single hour of peace. This idea may be illustrated by a page from the history of David Swan.

We have nothing to do with David Swan until we find him at the age of twenty on the main road from his home to the city of Boston where his uncle, a business man, is going to give him work in the store which he owns. It is enough to say that David was a native of the state of New Hampshire, that he was born of good parents and that he had received an ordinary school education. After traveling on foot from early morning until noon on a summer day, he felt tired and warm, and decided to sit down in the first convenient shady place and wait for the coming of the stage-coach, in order to ride the remaining distance. Thus he soon came upon a pleasant spot near a spring of water, surrounded by a group of shady trees. The place was quiet and cool. He kneeled down at the spring and drank deeply of the fresh water. Then he lay on the soft earth and resting his head upon a pair of trousers and some shirts, which he carried with him in the form of a small package, he fell into a deep sleep.

While he lay asleep in the shade, other people were wide awake and passing along the road, some in one direction, some in the opposite direction; some traveled on foot, others on horseback and in various kinds of vehicles. Some did not look to the right or left; others when they passed where David was sleeping glanced in David's direction but did not notice him. Some laughed when they saw how deeply he slept. A middle aged widow, when nobody else was near, stopped and looked at him tenderly and said to herself that the young fellow looked charming in his sleep. A minister, who was very much opposed to strong drink, saw him and thought he was drunk. The next Sunday he mentioned poor David in his church sermon as an awful example of the results of strong drink.

David had slept only a short time when a rich looking carriage, drawn by two fine horses, stopped directly in front of where he slept. One of the horses had injured its leg and the ness man and his wife got out of the carriage and decided to driver wished to let the horse rest for awhile. An elderly busi-

rest during this time under the shade of the trees. There they noticed the spring of water and David asleep alongside of it. They tried to walk lightly and to make as little noise as possible in order not to wake David.

"How deeply he sleeps," said the old gentleman. "How quietly and easily he breathes. If I could sleep as deeply as that, I would be very happy, for such sleep, without the help of sleeping medicines, indicates good health and a mind without troubles."

"And youth besides," said his wife. "Old people like us never sleep like that."

PART II

The old couple became more and more interested in the unknown youth who lay there so peacefully sleeping.

"It seems to me," said the woman at last to her husband, "that he strongly resembles our own dear son. Shall we wake him up?"

"For what purpose?" said the husband. "We know nothing of his character."

"That honest face," answered his wife in a quiet voice. "This innocent sleep!"

While the conversation was going on, David did not move, nor did the features of his face indicate that he knew that two people were looking at him with great interest. Nevertheless, Fortune was standing very close to him, for the old man and his wife were very rich. Their only son had recently died, and there was no one in their family to whom they wanted to leave all their money. In such cases, people sometimes do stranger things than to wake up a young man, accept him as their own son, and later make him the heir to all their riches.

"Shall we wake him up?" repeated the lady.

But suddenly the driver of the coach said, "We are ready now, Sir. The horse is rested."

The old couple stopped speaking suddenly, looked at each other with some surprise, and then hurried toward the coach. Once inside the coach, the whole idea of making David their son now seemed to them quite ridiculous, and they were surprised that such a strange thought could have come to their minds. Thus, the man began to tell his wife about the plan which he had, to leave all his money, when he died, for the establishment of a large charitable institution. Meanwhile, David went on enjoying his quiet sleep.

Not more than five minutes passed when a young girl came along. She had a light and easy step which showed at once the happiness of her spirit. She was also very pretty. She stopped to drink at the spring and was naturally surprised to find David sleeping there. At first she felt as if she had entered, without permission, into a gentleman's bedroom, and she was about to leave quietly when she saw an enormous bee buzzing around the head of the sleeper. Quickly but quietly, she attacked the bee with her handkerchief and drove him away. How sweet a picture! This good act completed, the girl looked tenderly for a moment at David.

"He is handsome," she said to herself.

But David did not move, nor did he smile. No look of appreciation or of welcome appeared upon his face. Perhaps the girl was the girl of his dreams, the girl with whom he might spend a life of happiness, if only he could awake and speak to her.

"How deeply he sleeps," said the girl.

She left, but she appeared thoughtful and now she did not move along the road as lightly or as happily as she had come.

Now this girl's father was the owner of a large store in the neighborhood, and he happened to be looking, at this time, for just such a young man as David Swan. If David had only awakened and had made the acquaintance of the pretty young girl, he probably would have become a clerk in her father's store, possibly have married the girl and later inherited the father's business. Here again, good fortune had come very close to David and had almost touched him but then disappeared.

PART III

The girl was hardly out of sight when two men turned from the road to stop a moment in the shade. Both had dark faces, and both wore caps which they pulled down well over their eyes. They wore old clothes. These men were robbers who were ready to steal anything they found and to kill anyone who might try to stop them. Seeing David asleep alongside the spring, one of them said to his companion:

"Look, do you see that package under his head?"

"Yes, perhaps he has a pocketbook or some money hidden inside of it," said the other. "Or perhaps he has some money in one of his pockets."

"But what if he wakes up?" said the first.

His companion pulled out a long knife from his belt and pointed it at David.

"This will take care of him,"he said.

They approached the sleeping David and prepared to remove the package from under his head. David continued to sleep tranquilly.

"You take the package. If he moves, I'll strike," said the man with the knife.

But, at this moment, a dog ran in from the road to drink at the spring. The dog paid no attention to the men nor to David but drank thirstily of the water. The men stopped suddenly and one of them drew a pistol from his pocket.

"Wait!" said the other man. "We can do nothing now. The

owner of the dog is probably close behind."

"Yes," said the other. "We'd better get out of here."

Thus the two men left as unexpectedly as they had come and they continued down the road. In a few minutes they had forgotten the entire event — and, of course, there was one less dark crime to be written against their names in the books of heaven — but of this they did not think for even a moment.

David slept, but no longer as quietly as at first. He had had an hour's peaceful sleep and was now more rested. He moved slightly and lay for a few minutes half asleep, half awake. Then suddenly in the distance there was a loud noise of approaching wheels. The stage coach was coming. David jumped up and ran out just in time to call to the driver.

"Hello, driver! Have you room for one more passenger?"

"There is room on top," answered the driver.

David climbed to the top of the coach and the driver started off. The coach moved quickly down the road, and David did not give even a final glance to the place where he had slept. He was thinking now of other things, of the life ahead of him. He had no memories of the place where he had rested because he had no knowledge of anything that had happened there. He did not know that Fortune had smiled on him and almost brought him great riches and a great love with perhaps a successful career in business. He did not know that he had been close to death at the point of a robber's knife — all within the space of one brief hour.

Thus it is that life deals with us in many strange ways. Fortunately, we do not know the many things that come close to us and pass us by without results. As was said in the beginning of this story, if we knew all the many possibilities of change in our fortune, life would be too full of hopes and fears, surprises and disappointments to permit us a single hour of peace.

Exercises Based on

DAVID SWAN

PART I

A. Answer These Questions:

1. Do we, according to the author, know little or much about the events which influence our daily lives? 2. Are there many or few possible changes in our daily fortune? 3. Do you feel that our destiny is definitely decided or that it is subject to many changes of chance and accident? 4. In what superstitions do you believe? 5. What superstitions are popular in your country? 6. Was David Swan a young man or an old man at the time of this story? 7. Was he on his way to the city of Boston or the city of Philadelphia? 8. In what state is the city of Boston located? 9. Is Boston larger or smaller than New York? 10. With what purpose was David Swan going to Boston? 11. Why did he decide to sit down in the first convenient place and wait for the stage-coach? 12. Are stage-coaches a modern or an old-fashioned means of transportation? 13. Were stage-coaches a rapid or a slow means of transportation? 14. Did this story take place recently or a long time ago? 15. What more modern means of transportation have replaced the stage-coach? 16. After David lay down alongside the spring, did he fall into a deep sleep or into a light sleep? 17. Do you generally sleep deeply or lightly? 18. Are you a light sleeper or a deep sleeper? 19. Do light sleepers wake up easily or with great difficulty? 20. Did David attract little attention or much attention from the people who passed along the road?

B. Vocabulary Drill. Choose The Correct Form:

1. The opposite of *shady* is (dark, cool, sunny, comfortable).
2. A synonym for *event* is (change, happening, accident, surprise).
3. The word *kneeled* is pronounced to rhyme with (killed, needed, solid, field).
4. A common synonym for *main* is (principal, native, remaining, fresh).

5. Give the opposites of these words: soft, cool, little, fresh, pleasant, early, close, often, full, deep, small, asleep, right, strong, drunk, short.

6. Give the past tense form and the past participial form of these verbs: sleep, lie, try, breathe, say, fall, kneel, sit, know.

7. *Sermons* are generally delivered by (a mailman, a minister or priest, parents, politicians).

8. *Elderly* means (young, middle-aged, rather old, rather charming).

9. What three different meanings can the word *spring* have in English?

10. Give the corresponding noun form of these adjectives: strong, young, weak, possible, tender, deep, shady, disappointed.

C. Use These In Sentences:

to pass by, to have nothing to do with, the main road (street), on foot, to wait for, to come upon, to kneel down, wide awake, for awhile.

PART II

A. Answer These Questions:

1. Were the couple who stopped to watch David Swan as he slept old or young? 2. Whom did they think he resembled? 3. Did David seem to them to have an honest or a dishonest face? 4. Did the old couple finally wake David up or did they let him sleep? 5. Were the old couple rich or poor? 6. Had their only son died recently or many years before? 7. Was David conscious or unconscious of their presence? 8. Why does the author say in this case that Fortune was standing very close to David? 9. Was the young girl who next passed by ugly or pretty? 10. Did she walk with a heavy step or with a light and easy step? 11. What insect did she attack with her handkerchief and drive away from David's head? 12. Did the girl think that David was ugly or handsome? 13. Did the girl wake David up or did she also let him sleep? 14. Was David conscious or unconscious of her presence? 15. If the bee had stung David, would David have awakened or would he have continued sleeping? 16. In such a case, was the girl wise or unwise to have driven away the bee? 17. Is the sting of a bee painful or painless? 18. Are bees supposed to be busy or lazy creatures? 19. What product do bees make by collecting the nectar

from different flowers? 20. If David had awakened and had met the pretty girl, what might have happened to him?

B. Vocabulary Drill. Choose The Correct Form:

1. The word *dear* is often used in everyday conversation with the meaning of (cheap, expensive, pretty, ugly, new).

2. The word *heir* is pronounced the same as (ear, air, or, are).

3. *Ridiculous* means (recent, intelligent, foolish, sudden).

4. Give the corresponding noun form of these verbs: establish, enjoy, accept, die, inherit, resemble, indicate, permit, complete, appreciate, appear.

5. *Meanwhile* means (sometimes, after awhile, in the meantime, now and then).

6. *At once* means (one time only, seldom, immediately, much later).

7. A common synonym for *handsome* is (elegant, strong, good-looking, happy).

8. The word *buzz* is pronounced to rhyme with (buys, does, goes, sneeze).

9. To *awaken* someone is to (put him to sleep, wake him up, surprise him, assist him).

10. If someone is *about to do something*, he (must do it, wants to do it, has just done it, is on the point of doing it).

C. Use These In Sentences:

at last, to wake up, to go on, to come along, at once, to be about to do something, to drive someone or something away, to say to oneself, to look for.

PART III

A. Answer These Questions:

1. Were the two men who next stopped at the spring good men or bad men? 2. Were they dressed well or in old clothes? 3. How did these men make their living? 4. What did they plan to do to David? 5. If David woke up, what did the one man threaten to do with his knife? 6. Why did the sudden entrance of a dog cause the men to change their plans about robbing David? 7. Was David conscious or unconscious of the presence of these men. 8. Was the appearance of the dog

a lucky or unlucky event for David? 9. What might have happened to David if the dog had not suddenly appeared? 10. What rather loud noise in the distance finally awakened David? 11. Had David had a restful or a restless sleep? 12. Did you sleep restfully or restlessly last night? 13. How many hours did you sleep last night? 14. How many hours of sleep does a person normally need? 15. How many hours of sleep do you personally require in order to feel well? 16. Was there room for David inside the coach or did he have to sit on top of the coach? 17. Did David look back at the place where he had slept or was he busy now thinking of other things? 18. Was he conscious or unconscious of the fact that he had attracted the attention of several people while he was asleep? 19. What was the author trying to explain in this story? 20. Do you consider this story more interesting or less interesting than some of the other stories? Why?

B. Vocabulary Drill. Choose The Correct Form:

1. A common synonym for *hardly* is (seldom, rarely, suddenly, scarcely).

2. A synonym for *robber* is (merchant, banker, lawyer, thief).

3. Which of these does a man use to hold up his trousers (garters, tie, belt, collar)?

4. *Tranquilly* means (loudly, peacefully, recently, thirstily).

5. Give the opposites of these words by adding the necessary prefix: happy, kind, expected, continue, possible, able, accustomed, appear, obey, regular, honest, convenient.

6. Give the corresponding adverb form of these adjectives: thirsty, hungry, easy, good, probable, hard, tranquil.

7. *We'd better leave* means that (we want to leave, we must leave, it is advisable that we leave).

8. The contraction *we'd* is pronounced to rhyme with (led, word, wide, need).

9. State these in contracted form: I will, we would, we had, I did not, I do not, he does not, we are, she is, I am, they will not, I have not, he has not, she would not, she had not.

10. *Brief* means (short, narrow, pretty, long).

C. Use These In Sentences:

inside of (outside of), to wake up, to pull out, to point at, to take care of, to pay attention to, had better, of course, to pass by.

THE SOCIETY OF RED-HEADED MEN

Conan Doyle

PART I

I called upon my friend Mr. Sherlock Holmes, the famous detective, one day last autumn and found him in conversation with a fat, middle-aged gentleman with bright red hair.

"Pardon me, Holmes," I said, "I didn't know — "

"Come in, Watson," said Holmes, pulling up a chair for me. "You could not have come at a better time."

"But perhaps you are busy."

"It doesn't matter," said Holmes. Then turning to the fat gentleman, he added, "Mr. Wilson, this man has been my companion and assistant in many of my most successful cases, and I have no doubt that he can help me in your case also."

The fat man rose from his chair and looked me over carefully.

"Do you mind starting your story again from the very beginning, Mr. Wilson?" Holmes asked. "I want Dr. Watson to hear all of the details, because it seems to me quite a singular case, unlike any other case in my experience. At present I cannot say whether there is any clear evidence of crime or not."

The fat gentleman pulled an old newspaper from his pocket and while he looked carefully down a column of advertisements, I took the opportunity to observe the man. I did not learn much from my inspection, however, because he looked like any other normal, middle-class Englishman. The only thing unusual about him was his bright red hair. Holmes, on the other hand, with his great powers of observation, was no doubt already able to give the whole history and background of the man just from looking at his clothes, his manners, and the numerous details of his general appearance.

"Here is the advertisement," said Mr. Wilson at last. "The whole thing began with this advertisement. You can read it for yourself, Sir."

I took the paper from him and read as follows: *To the Society of Red-Headed Men: There is now another position open in the Society of Red-Headed Men. The Society was founded some years ago with money left by Mr. E. Hopkins of Pennsylvania, U. S. A. The salary is four pounds a week for very little work. Any red-headed man over twenty-one may apply for the position. Ask for Duncan Ross at the offices of the Society of Red-Headed Men, 7 Fleet Street, Monday morning at eleven o'clock.*

"What does this mean?" I said after I had read it twice, trying to figure it out.

Holmes smiled and seemed to be in good spirits as was his custom when beginning a new and interesting case. "It is quite unusual, isn't it?" he said. "And now, Mr. Wilson, tell us something about your personal life and about the effect which this advertisement had upon your fortunes. You will note the date of the newspaper, Watson. This advertisement appeared exactly two months ago."

PART II

"Well, as I was telling you before," Mr. Wilson said, "I have a small business in which I lend money to people on jewels, clothing, and other personal things. My shop is located on Coburg Square, and I myself live in a few rooms in the same house behind my shop. Recently, business has not been very good, and it has been difficult for me even to make my living. I used to have two clerks, but now I have only one, and he fortunately works for about half pay. If I had to pay him more, I would not be able to keep him."

"What is the name of this young man who so kindly works for half pay?" asked Holmes.

"His name is Vincent Spaulding, and he is not so very young. I don't really know his age. But he is very capable and works very well. I often wonder why he doesn't leave me for a better position somewhere else."

"Yes, it is unusual," said Holmes. "Perhaps it is as unusual as your advertisement."

"Oh, he has his faults," said Wilson. "For example, he is very much interested in photography and spends very much time taking photographs. Then he always has to run down to the cellar and to spend much time there developing his pictures."

"He is still with you, I suppose," said Holmes.

"Oh, yes," said Wilson. "And, incidentally, it was he who first brought this advertisement to my attention. He came to the store one day with this very paper in his hand, saying:

" 'I certainly wish, Mr. Wilson, that I were a red-headed man.'

" 'Why?' I asked.

" 'Because here's another opening in the Society of Red-Headed Men. It's worth quite a lot of money to any man who can get it. They say that the salary is very good and that there is very little work connected with it. I surely wish that my hair would change color.'

" 'What kind of work is it?' I asked. You see, Mr. Holmes, I don't know much about what goes on in the world. I don't read the newspapers much and I usually stay at home every night.

" 'Haven't you ever heard of the Society of Red-Headed Men?' Spaulding asked with his eyes open.

" 'Never.'

" 'That's strange, because you yourself are red-headed and perhaps could obtain one of the positions.'

" 'And what are they worth?' I asked.

" 'Oh, only a couple of hundred pounds a year, but the work is light and a person can often do it and continue with his regular work at the same time.'

" 'Tell me all about it,' I said, because naturally I was interested in the possibility of getting that extra money.

" 'Well,' said he, 'You can see for yourself. The Society has a position open now, and there is the address with all the information. As I understand it, the Society was founded by an American millionaire, Mr. E. Hopkins, who was very strange in his manners. He himself was red-headed, and he had a great sympathy for all red-headed men. When he died he left an enormous fortune with instructions to form the society and give opportunities to red-headed men. It is always easy work and very good pay.'

PART III

" 'But,' said I, 'there are millions of red-headed men who could fill the position.'

" 'Not so many as you think. First, it is limited to Londoners and to adult men. This American was born in London and wished to do something for his home town. Then, also, I have heard that it is useless to ask for the position if your hair is light red or dark red, or anything except bright red like yours. I am sure, Mr. Wilson, that you could get the position easily if you were interested.'

"Now, it is a fact, gentlemen, that my hair is very bright red, and so I thought perhaps I might be able to earn this easy extra money. Vincent Spaulding seemed to know a lot about the entire matter, so I asked him to go with me the next day at eleven o'clock to the address given in the advertisement. Well, Mr. Holmes, I never hope to see such a sight again. It seemed that every man in London who had just a little red in his hair had come to Fleet street to get the job. The street was crowded and there was a line a block long waiting to get in. When I saw how many men were there, I wanted to give up the whole idea and to return home, but Vincent Spaulding insisted that I wait and he also pointed out that although there were many men with hair of every shade of red, there were very few who had really bright red hair like mine. Finally, he pulled and pushed me through the crowd until we arrived at the steps of the office. There was a double line of men, some going in with high hopes and some leaving in despair."

"Very, very interesting," said Holmes. "Please continue."

"There was nothing in the office except a few chairs and a table, behind which sat a small man with red hair even brighter than mine. He said a few words to each man as he came in but he always found some fault with each one. Getting the position did not seem to be an easy matter after all. However, when my turn came, the man seemed very much interested, and he closed the door behind me so that he could speak to me privately.

" 'This is Mr. Wilson,' said Vincent Spaulding, 'and he would like to fill the position which is open in the Society of Red-Headed Men.'

" 'Well, he seems to have the right color of hair,' the other answered. 'I don't know when I have seen anything so fine.' He then took a step backward, looked at me carefully for a minute, and then took my hand and shook it warmly.

" 'You will excuse me,' he went on, 'if I do something a little unusual.' And then suddenly he took hold of my hair with both his hands and pulled and pulled until I cried with pain. 'There is water in your eyes,' he said when he finished. 'That is fine. But, you see, we have to be very careful, for we have twice been fooled by artificial hair and once by paint.' He then went to the window and shouted to the crowd below that the position had been filled. There was a cry of disapproval, but soon one by one everyone disappeared until there was not a redhead in sight anywhere except the office manager and me.

PART IV

" 'My name is Duncan Ross,' he said, 'And I myself am a member of the Society of Red-Headed Men.'

"He then asked me whether I was a married man and, when I said that I was not, he said that the society really preferred married men who might later have children also with red hair, but perhaps they could accept me anyway. I then explained that I also was in business and was already busy during part of the day, but Vincent Spaulding then interrupted and said that he would be glad to take my place in the shop.

" 'What would be the hours?' I asked.

" 'Every day from ten until two.'

"Now my business is mainly done in the evenings anyway, and I knew that Vincent Spaulding could easily do the work during the day, so this seemed quite satisfactory.

" 'That would suit me very well,' I said. 'And what is the pay?'

" 'Four pounds a week.'

" 'And the work?'

" 'The work,' he said, 'is very simple. You have to be in this office everyday from ten to two, and if you leave at any time during these hours you immediately lose the position. During this time, each day, you simply have to copy pages from the encyclopedia. You start with the first volume, and you must bring your own pen, paper and ink. Will you be ready to begin tomorrow?'

" 'Certainly,' I said.

" 'Then, good-bye, Mr. Wilson, and let me say that I think you are very fortunate to have obtained such an excellent position.' We then shook hands, and I went home with my assistant in very fine spirits because of my good luck.

"By evening, however, when I began to think about the entire affair, I was less happy. It seemed to me rather ridiculous that someone was prepared to pay me all that money simply to sit four hours each day in a small office and copy words and sentences from the encyclopedia. I thought that somebody must be playing a joke on me. But Vincent Spaulding insisted that he was sure everything was all right, so the next day I decided to try it anyway. I bought paper, ink, and a pen and started out.

"Well, to my great surprise, everything turned out to be very satisfactory. The table was ready for me, and Mr. Duncan Ross was there waiting for me. He started me copying with the letter *A* and, from time to time, he would come in to see how I was doing. At two o'clock he wished me good-bye and said that he was very much pleased with my work.

"This went on day after day and on Saturday Mr. Ross came in and paid me my salary of four pounds. I was very happy. As time went on, Mr. Ross visited me less and less often until finally he seldom came at all except to pay me on Saturday. Of course, I could not leave the office at any time for fear of losing such a good position.

PART V

"Eight weeks passed away like this. I had copied almost everything under the letter *A* and was ready to begin with the letter *B* when suddenly the whole business came to an end."

"To an end?"

"Yes, Sir! One morning I went to work at ten o'clock as usual, but the door was closed and locked, and there was a sign on the door. Here, you can read it yourself." He held up a piece of white paper, on which was written the following:

The Society of Red-Headed Men Has Been Discontinued.
October 9

Sherlock Holmes and I read the paper carefully, looked at each other for a moment, and then both of us suddenly began to laugh.

"I do not see anything very funny in it," said Mr. Wilson a little angrily. "If you can do nothing except laugh at me, I can go somewhere else."

"No, no," said Holmes. "I am really very much interested in your case. It is most unusual. But it also has its humorous sides as well. But, tell me, what steps did you take next?"

"At first I did not know what to do. I went to some of the other offices in the same building, but no one knew anything about it. Then I went to the owner of the building. He said that he had never heard of the Society of Red-Headed Men. Then I asked him who Duncan Ross was. He said that the name was new to him.

" 'Well, the gentleman in Room Number 4,' I explained.

" 'The red-headed man?'

" 'Yes.'

" 'Oh,' said he. 'His name was William Morris. He was a lawyer and was using the office on a temporary basis until his own office was ready.'

" 'Where can I find him?'

" 'Oh, at his new office. He did tell me the address. Yes, 17 King Street.'

"I started off, but when I arrived at 17 King Street it was a large factory, and no one there had ever heard of either Mr. William Morris or Mr. Duncan Ross."

"And what did you do then?" asked Holmes.

"I simply went home and talked over the whole matter with my assistant, Mr. Vincent Spaulding. He said that he was sure that I would receive some communication by mail from the Society and that I should wait. But in the meantime I did not wish to lose such a good position, and, since I had heard that you, Mr. Holmes, sometimes help poor people with their problems, I decided to come and consult with you."

"You were very wise," said Holmes. "I am sure I can help you. Your case is an extremely unusual one and I think that perhaps it is a more serious matter than you realize."

"It is serious," said Wilson. "I have lost a position which paid me very well."

"Quite true," said Holmes. "And now tell me something about that assistant of yours, Vincent Spaulding. He interests me greatly. How long had he been working for you when he brought you that advertisement?"

"About a month."

"How did he come?"

"In answer to an advertisement."

"Was he the only person who answered the advertisement?"

"No, there were about a dozen."

"Why did you choose him?"

"Because he seemed capable and because he offered to work at about half the usual salary."

"What is he like, this Vincent Spaulding?"

"Small in stature, very quick in his manners, very little hair on his face although he must be about thirty years old. He also has a mark on his forehead."

Holmes sat up in his chair in great excitement. "I think I know him," he said. "Does he also have small holes in his ears in order to wear earrings?"

"Yes, he does."

"Well," said Holmes. "And he is still with you?"

"Yes, and he is still doing his work well."

"That will do, Mr. Wilson," Holmes said. "I shall be happy to give you an opinion within a day or two—probably by Monday."

PART VI

"Well, Watson," Holmes said after our visitor had left, "what do you think about it all?"

"I cannot understand it," I said. "It is certainly a mysterious business."

"As a rule," said Holmes, "the mysterious cases are usually the easy ones. The cases that look simple are often the most difficult."

"What are you going to do then?"

"I am going to smoke for about an hour and think about it." He sat comfortably in his chair, lit his pipe, and thus I left him alone for some time. Then suddenly, he jumped up and said:

"Come with me, Watson. There is a great violinist in town who is playing this afternoon. I am sure you can leave your patients for a few hours."

"I have little to do today," I said.

"Then put on your hat and coat and come with me. First, I am going by way of Coburg Square, where our friend Mr. Wilson has his shop. I want to take a look at the general neighborhood."

Thus we went first by subway as far as Aldersgate and from there we walked to Coburg Square, where we soon saw Wilson's shop. It was one of several two story houses, all rather dirty, and poorly kept. Sherlock Holmes stopped in front of the shop and looked it over carefully. Then he walked slowly up the street to the corner, examining all of the houses. Finally, he came back to Wilson's shop and pounded on the sidewalk with his cane. Then he went suddenly up to the door and knocked. A bright-looking, clean young man opened the door and asked him to step in.

"Thank you," said Holmes. "I only wished to ask how to reach the Strand Theatre from here."

"Three blocks right and four left," the young man answered, closing the door.

"A very clever fellow," said Holmes as we walked away. "He is, in my opinion, one of the most clever men in London—and he is also extremely brave. I have known something of him before."

"Apparently, Mr. Vincent Spaulding plays an important part in this mystery of the Society of Red-Headed Men," I said. "I suppose that you knocked at the door in order that you might see him."

"Not him."

"What then?"

"The knees of his trousers."

"And what did you see?"

"What I expected to see."

"Why did you pound upon the sidewalk?"

"My dear doctor, this is a time for observation, not for talk. We are in enemy territory and must be careful. Let us look around a little more."

We turned the corner and found ourselves on a very busy street, quite the opposite from the one on which Mr. Wilson's shop was located. There was much traffic and a constant stream of people hurrying along.

"Let me see," said Holmes, standing at the corner and looking down the street. "I should like to remember the exact order of the buildings here. There is first a tobacco shop, then a newspaper office, then the City Bank, next a restaurant, etc. And now I believe we have done our work and I have seen exactly what I expected to see. So it is time we had a sandwich and some coffee and then went to hear that violinist."

PART VII

Sherlock Holmes was a great lover of music, and he himself played the violin well and had even composed some music. All afternoon he sat listening to the music and was perfectly happy. Now he did not resemble at all the sharp, clever and brilliant detective that he was. He was quiet and dreamy now. But soon he would change, and, after such a period of rest and inactivity, he would be even more ready for the work at hand.

"You want to go home now, no doubt, Doctor," he said as we were leaving the theatre.

"Yes, I should like to," I said.

"And I have some business to do which will take some hours. This business at Coburg Square is serious.

"Someone is planning an important crime. I believe that we shall be in time to stop it. But today is Saturday, and that rather complicates matters. I shall want your help tonight."

"At what time?"

"Ten will be early enough."

"I shall be at your apartment at ten."

"Very well. And, Doctor, there may be a little danger, so put your revolver in your pocket." Then he smiled, turned away, and was soon lost in the crowd.

Now I do not think that I am more stupid than the next person, but whenever I was working with Sherlock Holmes I felt very much inferior. Here I had heard what he had heard. I had seen what he had seen, and yet from his words it was evident that he now clearly knew not only what had happened but what was going to happen. Yet to me the entire business was still very much confused. As I drove home to my house I thought it all over from the beginning of Mr. Wilson's story of the advertisement to the end but I could not figure it out. Where were we going that night and why did I have to carry a revolver?

It was a quarter past nine when I started from home, passed through the Park, and finally arrived at Holmes' apartment. As I entered the hall, I heard voices, and upon entering Holmes' room, I found him in conversation with two men, one of whom I recognized as Peter Jones, the official police inspector. The other was a long, thin-faced man who carried a black hat and wore a long frock coat.

"Well, now our party is complete," said Holmes, putting on his hat and coat. "Watson, I think you know Mr. Jones of the government police. Let me introduce you to Mr. Merryweather, who is going to be our companion in tonight's adventure."

"I hope our adventure does not prove to be a foolish one," said Mr. Merryweather a little sadly.

"You can have great confidence in Mr. Holmes, Sir," said Jones, the police officer, to Mr. Merryweather. "He has his own special methods which are, if he doesn't mind my saying so, a little too fantastic and theoretical at times, but he is a pretty good detective anyway."

"Oh, if you say so, Mr. Jones, it is all right," said Mr. Merryweather, "but it is Saturday night, and it is the first Saturday night in twenty-seven years that I have missed playing my usual game of cards."

PART VIII

"I think you will find," said Sherlock Holmes, "that you will play a much more interesting game than cards tonight. You, Mr. Merryweather, will win a great sum of money; and you, Jones, will catch the man you have been looking for so long."

"John Clay, the thief and murderer!" said Jones. "He's a young man, Mr. Merryweather, but he is the most clever man in the business, a very exceptional man! His grandfather was a royal duke, and he himself was educated in the University of Oxford. His brain is as clever as his fingers, and though we find signs of him in many crimes we have never been able to catch him."

"I hope I may have the pleasure of introducing you to him tonight," said Holmes. "Now, however, it is past ten o'clock, and it is time we started. If you two will take the first cab, Watson and I will follow in the second."

During the long drive Holmes did not talk much but did explain that Mr. Merryweather was a director of the City Bank and therefore very much interested in the night's adventure. He also said that he had invited Jones because he thought it was best to have a police officer with them.

Finally we reached the same busy street that we had visited that morning and we got out of our cabs directly in front of the City Bank. We went to a side door of the bank, which Mr. Merryweather opened for us with his keys and we then entered the bank.

We passed down a long hall which ended in a strong iron door. This door Mr. Merryweather also opened for us. Then we went down some stone steps and through another strong iron door which Merryweather opened. We were now in a deep stone cellar, where there were many boxes one on top of another.

"You are certainly safe from any robbery above," said Holmes.

"And also safe from robbery below," said Merryweather, striking the stone floor with his cane. "Good Heavens, it sounds as if it were empty below."

"I must really ask you to be a little more quiet," said Holmes severely. "You have almost placed our entire plan in danger. I must ask you to sit down on one of these boxes and wait patiently."

Mr. Merryweather took a place on one of the boxes and Holmes, meanwhile, kneeled down and began to examine carefully the stones of the floor with his magnifying glass. Soon he rose to his feet again and put his glass in his pocket.

"We have at least an hour to wait," he said, "for they will probably not try to do anything until after Mr. Wilson has gone to bed. Then they will not lose a minute, for if they do their work quickly, they will have more time to escape. You know, of course, Dr. Watson, that we are in the cellar of the City Bank, and Mr. Merryweather can tell you why London thieves are very much interested in entering the place at present."

"It is our French gold," said Merryweather. "About two months ago we borrowed about 30,000 pounds from the Bank of France. It is located in these very boxes on which we are sitting."

"And now it is time that we prepare our plans," said Holmes. "I expect that within an hour we may expect some action. We must put out the light and remain in the dark behind these boxes. When they come, I will turn my light on them, and we will jump on them."

PART IX

I placed my gun on top of a box and stood quietly waiting. It was now completely dark and there was a feeling of tenseness and anxiety among us.

"There is only one way for them to escape from here," said Holmes. "That is back through Wilson's place. I hope that you have done what I asked you, Jones."

"I have an inspector and two officers waiting at the front door."

"Then we have stopped all the holes. And now we must be silent and wait."

It seemed that we waited a very long time. Actually, it was only about an hour, but it seemed to me that the night must have gone and that morning would arrive soon. My legs were tired, for I was afraid to change my position or to make any noise. Then suddenly I saw a light along the floor. At first it was very small but soon it grew longer. It came from the side of one of the stones which formed the floor. There was next a long pause and then suddenly there was a loud noise as one of the stones was turned over. A strong light now came from the hole where the stone had lain. Soon the head of a young man appeared. The man then put his hands on the side of the hole and pulled himself up. He now stood on the side of the hole. He then reached down and helped a second man to climb up out of the hole. This second man had bright red hair similar to Mr. Wilson's.

"All clear!" the first man said. "Have you the bags and the tools? Heavens! Jump, Archie! Run!"

Sherlock Holmes had jumped out and thrown himself upon the first man. The second man jumped down into the hole as Jones tried to catch him. The first man had a revolver in his hand but Holmes knocked it out of his hand with his walking stick.

"It's no use, John Clay," said Holmes. "You have no chance at all."

"So I see," the other answered coolly. "But my companion has escaped."

"There are three men waiting for him at the door of Wilson's shop," said Holmes.

"You have done everything very completely."

"You also did everything very completely," said Holmes. "Your idea of the red-headed society was very clever."

Jones then came forward and placed handcuffs on Clay. There was an angry exchange of words between them, but Jones finally led him away as we followed them from the cellar.

"Really, Mr. Holmes," said Mr. Merryweather, "I do not know how the bank can thank you or repay you. There is no doubt that you have defeated two very dangerous criminals, and also saved the bank a great deal of trouble and expense."

"It gives me personal pleasure to have been able to capture John Clay," said Holmes. "This is sufficient satisfaction for me. I have had a few small expenses in the matter, and the bank can repay me for those."

PART X

An hour later Holmes and I were sitting in his apartment in Baker Street, drinking a glass of wine.

"You see, Dr. Watson," said Holmes, "it was clear from the beginning that the only purpose of the fantastic *Society of Red-Headed Men* was to get poor Mr. Wilson away from his shop for several hours each day. It was a strange way of arranging it, but it would be difficult to imagine a better one. I suppose the method was suggested to Clay's clever mind by the fact that his companion and Mr. Wilson both had bright red hair. They had to pay Wilson four pounds a week to copy from the encyclopedia but, after all, they were playing for a much greater sum of money. The first thing that made me suspicious was the fact that Mr. Wilson's assistant offered to work for half pay. Thus he must have had a very strong motive for wanting the position."

"But how did you figure out what the motive was?"

"Well, Mr. Wilson's business was a small one. Therefore, there was nothing in the house which they wanted. It must be something outside the house. What could it be? The assistant was very much interested in photography and spent much time in the cellar. The cellar? What was he doing in the cellar? I could think of nothing else except that they were making a tunnel to some place.

"I, of course, surprised you when we first visited Wilson's shop by pounding on the sidewalk with my stick. But I wanted to find out whether the tunnel ran behind or in front of the shop. Further, when I rang the bell and the assistant answered the door, I saw from his trousers that he had been working on his knees because his trousers were worn and dirty at that point. The only problem was to find out the direction of the tunnel. When we walked around the corner and saw the City Bank, I knew immediately that their plan was probably to run a tunnel to the cellar of this bank."

"But how could you tell that they would try to enter the bank tonight?"

"When they closed the offices of the *Society of Red-Headed Men* I knew that their work must be almost finished because they were no longer interested in Mr. Wilson's absence from the shop. But it was necessary that they act soon because the gold might possibly be moved somewhere else. Saturday would be better than any other day because the bank is closed on Sunday, and it would give them two days in which to escape."

"You figured it all out beautifully," I said.

"Oh, such little problems always interest me," said Holmes. "They are really very simple, and they help me to pass the time."

Exercises Based on

THE SOCIETY OF RED-HEADED MEN

PART I

A. Answer These Questions:

1. What is the name of the famous detective mentioned in this story? 2. What other famous stories about this detective have you read, either in English or translated into your native language? 3. Was Sherlock Holmes an American or an Englishman? 4. Is Dr. Watson an important person in all the Sherlock Holmes stories or is he only the one who tells the story? 5. Does the story open in the apartment of Sherlock Holmes or in the apartment of Dr. Watson? 6. Why had the red-headed man come to call on Sherlock Holmes? 7. What strange advertisement did he bring with him? 8. What was the Society of Red-Headed Men? 9. Had the society been founded by an Englishman or an American? 10. Do many people or few people have red hair? 11. What color hair have you? 12. Did the gentleman who called on Mr. Holmes at the beginning of this story have bright red hair or dark red hair? 13. Could any one apply for the position mentioned in the advertisement, or was it limited to red-headed men? 14. In what city does this story take place?

B. Vocabulary Drill. Choose The Correct Form:

1. To *call upon* someone is to (telephone him, visit him, criticize him, admire him).

2. A common synonym for *autumn* is (spring, duty, necessity, fall).

3. With which of these words does the contraction *I'll* rhyme: still, steel, style, stole?

4. It *doesn't matter* means that it (is necessary, is useless, is not important).

5. Give the past tense form and the past participial form of these verbs: rise, find, say, seem, take, learn, begin, read, ask, smile, tell. Which of these verbs are *regular verbs* and which are *irregular verbs?*

6. *Do you mind starting* means (do you want to start, do you object to starting, are you accustomed to starting).

7. A *singular* case is (an old case, a typical case, an unusual case, a difficult case).

8. When we say that the society was *founded,* we mean that the society was (located, ended, established, continued).

9. Give the corresponding noun form of these verbs: advertise, appear, apply, observe, inspect, assist, succeed, converse.

10. Distinguish in use between the two words *affect* and *effect.*

C. Use These In Sentences:

to call upon, to pull up a chair, to look over, at present, on the other hand, at last, no doubt, to figure out, as follows, to be in good spirits.

PART II

A. Answer These Questions:

1. Was Mr. Wilson a business man or a professional man? 2. Is a lawyer a business man or a professional man? 3. Did Mr. Wilson say that it had been easy or difficult for him to earn a living? 4. Did Mr. Wilson's assistant work for double pay or for half pay? 5. Was Sherlock Holmes an efficient or an inefficient detective? 6. Why did Mr. Wilson's assistant spend much time in the cellar of the shop? 7. What hobby was he presumably practicing there? 8. What is a hobby? 9. Who had first brought the advertisement to the attention of Mr. Wilson? 10. Was the position offered in the advertisement an

easy or a difficult one? 11. In what kind of business was Mr. Wilson? 12. Did Mr. Wilson employ many assistants in his shop or only one? 13. Was Mr. Wilson's assistant a capable worker or a poor one? 14. Does a capable worker work efficiently or inefficiently? 15. What is the noun form of the word *efficient?*

B. Vocabulary Drill. Choose The Correct Form:

1. The opposite of *to lend* is to (need, borrow, steal, beg, save).
2. *Jewels* are (old coins, stamps, fancy earrings, precious stones).
3. A synonym for *recently* is (rarely, suddenly, a long time ago, lately).
4. I *wonder* means that I (am surprised, like to travel, read a lot, would like to know).
5. *Unusual* means (interesting, strange, easy, difficult).
6. How many syllables does each of the following words contain and on which syllable does the accent fall: photography, salary, fortunately, changed, wished, connected, opening?
7. A common equivalent for *incidentally*, used in everyday conversation, is (now and then, after a while, by the way, up to now).
8. *Extra* generally means (new, difficult, additional, heavy, light).
9. Give the opposites of these words: light, great, open, easy, first, often, better, small, few, behind, old, half pay.
10. In which of these words is the letter *s* pronounced like *s* and in which is it pronounced like *z*: is, his, so, as, has, yes, first, ask, goes, eyes, was, address, perhaps, works, runs?

C. Use These In Sentences:

to make a living, used to have, somewhere else, to be interested in, to spend time, to stay at home, to bring to one's attention, to go on, to hear of, to be red-headed.

PART III

A. Answer These Questions:

1. Was the position in the Society of Red-Headed Men limited to Londoners or to New Yorkers? 2. Of what country is London the capital? 3. What is the capital of the United States? 4. Did Mr. Wilson's assistant think it would be easy or difficult for Mr. Wilson

to get the position? 5. Was Mr. Wilson interested or uninterested in earning a little extra money? 6. Did many men or few men apply for the position? 7. Did Mr. Spaulding insist that Mr. Wilson remain and try for the position or did he insist that they leave? 8. Was the man in the office pleased with all the applicants or did he always find some fault with each one? 9. Was he interested or uninterested in Mr. Wilson? 10. Was he satisfied or dissatisfied with the color of Mr. Wilson's hair? 11. Did Mr. Wilson have bright red hair or dark red hair? 12. Was the position open to any man with red hair or only to men with bright red hair? 13. Why did the man suddenly take hold of Mr. Wilson's hair and pull it strongly? 14. Did Mr. Wilson cry with delight or with pain? 15. Was Mr. Wilson's red hair real or artificial?

B. Vocabulary Drill. Choose The Correct Form:

1. *Whole* means (a hole, new, entire or complete, in part).

2. Distinguish in meaning between *block,* used as a noun, and *block,* used as a verb.

3. A synonym for *however* is (nevertheless, seldom, in addition, by the way).

4. A *fault* is a (virtue, defect, good salary, bright color).

5. Give the opposites of these words: backward, careful, light red, warmly, pull, finish, right, question, open, long, easy, easily, useless, double, high, small, few, behind, private.

6. Give the opposites of these words by adding the necessary prefix: appear, approve, happy, kind, usual, necessary, possible, polite, regular.

7. To be *fooled* is to be (amused, pleased, deceived, called a fool).

8. *Artificial* means (brightly colored, expensive, not real or genuine, cheap).

9. State these phrases in negative form: it seemed, he could get, I have heard, he pointed, I saw, I asked, there were, he does it well, he pushed and pulled.

10. Which one of these words is not spelled correctly: despair, advertisment, artificial, disapproval, unusual, insisted?

C. Use These In Sentences:

to be born, to give up, to arrive at, to find fault with, after all, to look at, to go on, to take hold of, one by one.

PART IV

A. Answer These Questions:

1. Why did the Society of Red-Headed Men prefer married men as members? 2. Did the position require long hours or short hours? 3. What was the work required by the position? 4. Was this work easy or difficult? 5. From what book did Mr. Wilson have to copy? 6. Was Mr. Wilson pleased or displeased at having gotten such a fine position? 7. With what letter of the alphabet did he have to begin his copying work? 8. How many letters are there in the English alphabet? 9. Was Mr. Wilson happy or unhappy on Saturday when he received his salary of four pounds? 10. As time went on, did Mr. Ross visit him less and less or more and more? 11. To Mr. Wilson's surprise did everything turn out to be very satisfactory or very unsatisfactory? 12. Roughly, what hours did Mr. Wilson have to work? 13. Was the pay adequate or inadequate? 14. Was the work interesting or dull? 15. With what volume of the encyclopedia did he have to begin copying?

B. Vocabulary Drill. Choose The Correct Form:

1. That would *suit me* means that would (frighten me, delay me, be convenient for me, help me).

2. You *have to* be there means that you (should be there, must be there, may be there, ought to be there).

3. How many syllables does each of the following words contain and on which syllables does the accent fall: encyclopedia, volume, fortunate, obtained, ridiculous, wished?

4. Which of the following past tense forms are pronounced as words of one syllable and which are pronounced as words of two syllables: turned, looked, played, wished, suited, pleased, seemed, worked, started?

5. A common synonym for *fortunate* is (easy, recent, simple, lucky).

6. *From time to time* means (often, now and then, never, fortunately).

7. This *went on* means that this (began, stopped, continued, occurred).

8. A synonym for *seldom* is (rarely, recently, lately, frequently).

9. There is a slight difference in use between *wages* and *salary*. When do we use *salary* and when do we use *wages?*

10. Distinguish in meaning between *pound,* used as a noun, and *pound,* used as a verb.

C. Use These In Sentences:

to be in business, to suit a person, to shake hands, because of, to think about, to play a joke on, to turn out, from time to time, day after day.

PART V

A. Answer These Questions:

1. Did Mr. Wilson spend eight years or only eight weeks doing his copying work? 2. Did the work terminate gradually or suddenly? 3. What sign did Mr. Wilson find on the door of the office one morning when he went to work? 4. When Sherlock Holmes and Dr. Watson read this sign, did they suddenly begin to cry or to laugh? 5. Was Mr. Wilson pleased or annoyed when Holmes and Watson laughed at his story of the sign? 6. When Mr. Wilson went to the owner of the building to inquire about Mr. Ross, did the owner know anything of Mr. Ross or was he entirely ignorant of such a person? 7. Why had Mr. Wilson finally come to consult Sherlock Holmes? 8. Did Sherlock Holmes think that he was able or unable to help Mr. Wilson? 9. How had Mr. Wilson come to employ his assistant, Mr. Spaulding? 10. Did Holmes claim to know Mr. Spaulding or was Mr. Spaulding entirely unknown to him? 11. Had Mr. Ross used the name of Ross when renting the office or had he used another name? 12. What do you think was his purpose in using a fictitious name? 13. What different types of people sometimes use fictitious names? 14. What is your last name? Your first name? 15. Is the mother's family name used as part of one's name in English or is only the father's family name used?

B. Vocabulary Drill. Choose The Correct Form:

1. To *talk over* something is to (argue about it, discuss it, avoid talking about it).

2. Read the following sentences and then explain the two different meanings which the word *funny* has in present-day English: 1. John

told a *funny* story, at which we all laughed. 2. During the night I heard a *funny* noise in the next room.

3. Give the corresponding adverb form of these adjectives: angry, happy, easy, temporary, wise, extreme, serious, good.

4. A synonym for *in the meantime* is (nevertheless, meanwhile, still, yet).

5. The opposite of *temporary* is (unusual, permanent, serious, excited).

6. The word *wise* is pronounced to rhyme with (ice, eyes, is, ease, ace).

7. The word *lose* is pronounced to rhyme with (loose, loss, chose, chews).

8. Distinguish in meaning between *to hear of* a person and *to hear from* a person.

9. *What is he like* means (what does he do for a living, what does he like, what is his description).

10. Give the corresponding noun form of these verbs: excite, assist, advertise, lose, decide, consult, realize, communicate, choose.

C. Use These In Sentences:

to come to an end, to hold up, to look at each other, to start off, to hear of, to talk over, by mail, in the meantime, to be like.

PART VI

A. Answer These Questions:

1. Did the case seem simple or mysterious to Dr. Watson? 2. Why did Sherlock Holmes sit down for a while and smoke his pipe? 3. Did he later invite Dr. Watson to hear a violinist or a pianist play? 4. Why did Sherlock Holmes and Dr. Watson later go to the neighborhood of Wilson's shop? 5. Did they find the shop to be large and impressive or rather dirty and poorly kept? 6. Why do you suppose Holmes pounded on the sidewalk with his cane? 7. Who answered when Holmes knocked at the door of Wilson's shop? 8. Did Holmes say that he had wanted to see Vincent Spaulding or only the knees of his trousers? 9. Why do you suppose Holmes was interested in seeing the knees of Vincent Spaulding's trousers? 10. What important build-

ings did Holmes and Watson find on the street next to that on which Wilson's shop was located? 11. After taking note of the buildings, did Holmes and Watson go home or did they go to hear a great violinist? 12. What musical instruments are you able to play? 13. What is your favorite musical instrument? 14. Can you read music? 15. Does it take longer to learn to play the piano or the violin?

B. Vocabulary Drill. Choose The Correct Form:

1. *As a rule* means (seldom, according to law, in general, never).

2. Give the corresponding noun form of these adjectives: mysterious, difficult, comfortable, dirty, brave, important.

3. A *shop* is a (restaurant, newspaper office, small store, department store).

4. Pick out the silent letters in each of these words: walk, talk, knock, knee, neighbor, answer, Wednesday, half, listen, wrong, honest.

5. A synonym for *brave* is (nervous, courageous, timid, strong).

6. The word *knees* is pronounced to rhyme with (niece, peace, sneeze, snows).

7. *Constant* means (occasional, rare, mysterious, steady or continuous).

8. Use each of these words in sentences, once as a noun and once as a verb: turn, knock, smile, cry, look, part, step, wish, promise, rest.

9. A *bright looking* person is (a good looking person, a clean looking person, an intelligent looking person).

10. Give the past tense form and the past participial form of these verbs: come, say, think, ask, close, sit, leave, jump, put, come, have, step, know, see. Which of these are "irregular verbs" and which are "regular verbs"?

C. Use These In Sentences:

to think about as a rule, to jump up, to put on, by way of, to take a look at, as far as, to look over, to step in, to look around.

PART VII

A. Answer These Questions:

1. Was Holmes interested or uninterested in music? 2. What musical instrument did he play well? 3. What is the difference between a

composer and an author? 4. Who is your favorite composer? 5. Did Holmes consider the case in question a serious or an unimportant one? 6. Did he feel that they would be able or unable to prevent the crime? 7. When Dr. Watson was working with Sherlock Holmes on a case, did he always feel inferior or superior to Holmes? 8. When Dr. Watson went to Holmes' apartment that evening what men did he find there in conversation with Holmes? 9. Did Mr. Merryweather seem enthusiastic or unenthusiastic about the night's adventure? 10. How had he spent every Saturday night during the past twenty-seven years? 11. What card games do you know how to play? 12. What card games are most popular in the United States today? 13. Did Holmes believe that someone was planning an important or an unimportant crime? 14. Was the case entirely clear or entirely mysterious to Dr. Watson? 15. Was it apparently clear or still mysterious to Holmes at this point?

B. Vocabulary Drill. Choose The Correct Form:

1. *Perfectly happy* means (fairly happy, rather happy, completely happy, not at all happy).

2. Give the corresponding noun form of these verbs: complicate, compose, confuse, advertise, converse, arrive, enter, recognize, inspect, introduce.

3. Use each of the following in sentences, once using the word as a noun and once as a verb: change, hope, mind, plan, help, figure, doubt, hand, face, crowd, look.

4. Distinguish in meaning between *in time* and *on time.*

5. A *revolver* is a (revolving door, pistol, pocketbook, advertisement).

6. It was *evident* means that it was (serious, apparent, late, humorous).

7. Give the opposites of these words: inferior, inactive, seldom, much, important, enter, find, long, thin-faced, first, sharp, quiet.

8. *Pretty good* means (very good, fairly good, exceptionally good, not good).

9. Distinguish in meaning between these idiomatic phrases: to put on something, to put off something, to put something away.

10. *At times* means (often, occasionally, seldom, soon).

C. Use These In Sentences:

all afternoon, at all, to take time, in time, to think over, to figure out, to arrive at, to have confidence in, at times.

PART VIII

A. Answer These Questions:

1. Was Mr. Jones very much interested or was he uninterested in catching the criminal, John Clay? 2. Was John Clay a clever or a stupid fellow? 3. Is it easier for the police to catch a stupid criminal or a clever one? 4. Was John Clay an educated or an uneducated man? 5. Was Mr. Merryweather another police officer or a director of the City Bank? 6. Did they enter the bank by the front door or did Mr. Merryweather open a side door for them? 7. With what were the boxes which they found there filled? 8. Had the money been borrowed from the Bank of France or from the Bank of America? 9. Is a bank generally a safe or an unsafe place in which to leave money? 10. Are banks generally well protected or poorly protected against robberies? 11. What famous American banks have you heard of? 12. Do you often or seldom have occasion to visit a bank? 13. Do you have a savings account in some bank? 14. Is it easy or difficult to borrow money from a bank? 15. Was the bank in this story well protected or poorly protected against robbery?

B. Vocabulary Drill. Choose The Correct Form:

1. A great *sum* is a great (event, crowd, amount, reception).
2. A common synonym for *cab* is (wagon, girl friend, taxi, plane).
3. The word *passed* is pronounced to rhyme with (waste, least, fast, fist).
4. Use each of these correctly in sentences: rob, robber, robbery.
5. A *hall* is a (large room, corridor, iron door, stone cellar).
6. Distinguish in meaning between *safe,* used as an adjective, and *safe,* used as a noun.

7. A *magnifying* glass makes things look (prettier, smaller, larger, duller).

8. The opposite of *to borrow* is to (need, lend, wait, arrive on time).

9. The word *light* may be used as a noun, a verb, and an adjective without any change in form. Give sentences showing these three different uses of *light*.

10. In which of these words is the letter *s* pronounced like *s* and in which is it pronounced like *z*: rose, glass, plans, lose, loose, this, these, keys, us, pass, steps, boxes, Holmes, he's?

C. Use These In Sentences:

to look for, to be interested in, to get out of, in front of, as if, in danger, to sit down, at least, to go to bed, within an hour.

PART IX

A. Answer These Questions:

1. Did Holmes and his party await quietly or noisily the approach of the criminals? 2. Was the room in which they waited completely dark or completely light? 3. Was there any way of escape for the criminals or had all ways been blocked by the police? 4. Did a light suddenly appear along the floor or along the ceiling? 5. Did one of the police officers or one of the criminals soon appear in the opening in the floor? 6. How had the criminals reached the bank from Wilson's shop? 7. Do you think Mr. Wilson was aware or was ignorant of their activities? 8. What were the criminals planning to do in the cellar of the bank? 9. Was Mr. Merryweather very grateful or ungrateful to Holmes for his good work in defeating the criminals? 10. What did Jones place on the wrists of John Clay before leading him away? 11. Where have you met John Clay previously in this story? 12. When Holmes threw himself upon John Clay, what did the other criminal do? 13. Did the second man escape or were there policemen waiting for him at the door of Wilson's shop? 14. Are handcuffs placed on the wrists or on the ankles of a person? 15. Do handcuffs make it easy or difficult for a criminal to escape?

B. Vocabulary Drill. Choose The Correct Form:

1. *Actually* means (very soon, really, frequently, often).

2. Give the past tense form and the past participial form of these verbs: seem, lie, see, grow, put, stand, climb, do, come, lead, pay, give, save. Which of these are "regular verbs" and which are "irregular verbs"?

3. *It's no use* means that it is (no fun, useless, too late, of no importance).

4. A *walking stick* is another name for a (canoe, cane, policeman's club, clever thief).

5. Which of these often use *handcuffs* in their work (lawyers, doctors, dentists, policemen)?

6. Give the opposites of these words: forward, coolly, strong, appear, pull, bright-red, top, few, small, follow.

7. In which of these words is the final letter *d* pronounced like *d* and in which is it pronounced like *t*: stopped, used, escaped, placed, appeared, turned, knocked?

8. To *repay* someone is to (lend him money, borrow from him, pay him back, fail to pay him).

9. A common synonym for *sufficient* is (enough, some, sudden, seldom).

10. Give the corresponding noun form of these adjectives: tense, anxious, dangerous, angry, similar, silent, dark.

C. Use These In Sentences:

on top of, at first, to turn over, to pull up, to climb up out of, to jump out (up, down), to throw oneself upon, to knock something down (off, out of), to be no use, to come forward.

PART X

A. Answer These Questions:

1. What, according to Mr. Holmes, was the purpose of the fantastic Society of Red-Headed Men? 2. Do you consider the idea of the Society of Red-Headed Men a clever one or a stupid one? 3. What first made Holmes suspicious of Mr. Wilson's assistant? 4. Is it usual

or unusual for a man to work for half pay? 5. What made Holmes think that the criminals were interested in something outside of Wilson's house rather than something inside his house? 6. In what part of Mr. Wilson's shop did his assistant John Clay spend very much time? 7. Was Clay working at photography in the cellar or constructing a tunnel? 8. To what place was he constructing a tunnel? 9. What did Holmes learn from seeing the knees of John Clay's trousers when Clay answered the door? 10. Who finally proved to be the more clever in this story, the criminals or Sherlock Holmes? 11. What was the purpose of the criminals in constructing a tunnel? 12. Why did they close the offices of the Society of Red-Headed Men? 13. Who suggested the idea of the "Society" to John Clay? 14. Why was it necessary for the criminals to act soon? 15. Why did they consider Saturday the best day to commit the crime?

B. Vocabulary Drill. Choose The Correct Form:

1. *Fantastic* means (real, well arranged, difficult, unreal or unbelievable).

2. Give the corresponding noun form of these verbs: imagine, suggest, arrange, suspect, enter, satisfy, suppose.

3. *Wine* is generally made from (potatoes, grapes, vines, seeds).

4. Give the corresponding noun form of these adjectives: absent, present, necessary, possible, beautiful, probable, suspicious, dangerous, strong.

6. Pick out the silent letters in these words: answer, should, would, wrong, walk, talk, knee, know, listen, doubt.

7. A *tunnel* generally passes (through a woods, over a river, underground, up a hill).

8. Distinguish in meaning between *worn* and *worn out.*

9. A common synonym for *trousers* is (jacket, vest, pants, skirt).

10. With which of these words does the contraction *I'd* rhyme: laid, lid, lied, lead?

C. Use These In Sentences:

after all, half pay, to figure out, to be interested in, nothing else, to find out, somewhere else, no longer, to pass the time.

THE GREAT STONE FACE

Nathaniel Hawthorne

PART I

One afternoon, when the sun was going down, a mother and her little boy sat at the door of their home, talking about the Great Stone Face. They had only to raise their eyes, and there it was, easily to be seen, although miles away, with the sunshine making clear all its features.

And what was the Great Stone Face?

Deep among a group of high mountains, there was a valley so wide that it contained many thousand inhabitants. Some of the inhabitants lived in small, poor houses with deep woods all around them. Others had their homes in comfortable farm houses, and they cultivated the earth and raised vegetables and fruits. Others lived together in villages or towns, and there was even a factory here and there. The inhabitants of this valley, in other words, were numerous and of many modes of life. But all of them, grown people and children, were familiar with the Great Stone Face, although some of them, it seemed, were able to distinguish more clearly than their neighbors this great natural phenomenon.

The Great Stone Face, then, was a work of Mother Nature, formed on the side of a mountain by some immense rocks, which had been thrown together in such a position that, when seen from a distance, they seemed to resemble the features of a human face. There was the broad forehead, more than a hundred feet in height, the long nose, the heavy lips, which, if they could have spoken, would have caused a noise like thunder through the valley. True it is, that if a person approached too near, he lost the outline of the gigantic face and saw only some immense rocks. But as he went farther back, the outline became more and more clear until the face seemed positively alive.

It was considered fortunate for children to be able to grow up to become men and women with the Great Stone Face always before their eyes, for the features of the face were noble and kind. It was an education only to look at it. According to the belief of many people, the land of the valley was especially fertile because of the influence of the kind face which was continually shining over it.

As we said before, a mother and her little son sat at the door of their home looking at the Great Stone Face and talking about it. The child's name was Ernest.

"Mother," he said, looking at the Great Stone Face, "I wish it could speak, for it looks so kind that I am sure the voice would be very pleasant. If I ever meet a man with such a face, I am sure I shall like him very much."

"There is a tradition in the valley which says that someday a great man will appear with exactly such a face," said his mother. Then his mother told Ernest a story that her own mother had told her, a story of things to come in the future; a story, however, so old that even the Indians who previously inhabited this valley had heard it from their fathers before them. The story was that, at some future day, a child would be born in this valley who would become the greatest and most noble person of his time. His face, when he became a man, would exactly resemble the Great Stone Face. Many people still believed in this story and waited for the coming of the great man, but others, who had seen more of this world, thought that it was only a foolish story. In any case, the great man of the tradition had not yet appeared.

"Oh, dear mother!" cried Ernest. "I do hope that I shall live to see him some day."

"Perhaps you may," said his mother, a kind and thoughtful woman.

PART II

And Ernest never forgot the story which his mother told him. It was always in his mind when he looked at the Great Stone Face. Ernest was a good boy, and he spent much time helping his mother, assisting her much with his little hands and more with his loving heart. In this manner, from a happy but quiet child, he grew up to be a strong young man, sun-browned from his hard labor in the fields but with more intelligence than is seen in many boys who go to famous schools. Yet Ernest had had no teacher, except that the Great Stone Face became a teacher to him. When his day's work was done, Ernest would look at it for hours until he began to imagine that those enormous features recognized him and gave him a smile of kindness and understanding in return.

About this time there went a rumor throughout the valley that the great man, as predicted many years ago and who was supposed to resemble the Great Stone Face, had appeared at last. It seems that many years before, a young man who had been born in the valley left his home and went to live in a distant city near the sea. Later he went into business. His business grew and grew until he became very rich and was the owner of many ships. These ships brought him goods from all corners of the earth and also brought him great wealth until it seemed that everything he touched turned into money. And when at last Mr. Gathergold—or so he was called—became so rich that it would have taken him a hundred years just to count his money, he began to think of his native valley, and he decided to return and end his days where he was born. Accordingly, he sent an architect to build him an enormous house, suitable for a man as rich as he.

People in the valley were already saying that Mr. Gathergold was the man, according to the tradition, that everyone had been waiting for. They said that he clearly resembled the Great Stone Face. People were more ready to believe this when they saw the magnificent home which he was building in the place where originally stood the old weather-beaten farm house of Mr. Gathergold's father. The exterior was of marble, so white that it resembled snow. There was a long porch and enormous pillars. It was a palace, suitable for any king. No one had been permitted to see the interior of the house but it was reported to be even richer and more wonderful than the exterior. Finally the mansion was finished. Many fine pieces of furniture arrived, and there followed an entire army of both black and white servants. Mr. Gathergold himself was expected to arrive late in the afternoon. Our friend Ernest, meanwhile, had been deeply moved by the idea that the great man, the noble man, the man of the tradition, after so many years was going to appear at last. Although still only a very young man, Ernest knew that there were many ways in which Mr. Gathergold, with his vast riches, could help the people of the valley and become as important an influence upon their lives as the smile of the Great Stone Face. Ernest did not doubt for a minute that at last he was going to see a living resemblance to the noble features of the Great Stone Face.

"Here he comes," cried a group of people who, like Ernest, had come to see the arrival. "Here comes the great Mr. Gathergold."

A carriage with four horses came around the corner of the road. Inside the carriage sat Mr. Gathergold. His skin was old, yellow, and wrinkled. He had a low forehead, small, sharp eyes, and thin lips which he made still thinner by pressing them tightly together.

"He looks exactly like the Great Stone Face," shouted the people. "The prediction has come true, and we have the great man at last."

What greatly confused Ernest was the fact that the people really seemed to believe that Mr. Gathergold resembled the Great Stone Face. Ernest turned away from the carriage and looked up the valley where in the last rays of the afternoon sun he could still distinguish the noble features of the Great Stone Face. The kindly lips seemed to say:

"He will come! Do not fear, Ernest! The great man will come."

PART III

The years went on and Ernest grew to be a man. He attracted little attention in the valley because there was nothing unusual in his mode of life except that when the day's work was over he liked to sit and look in the distance at the Great Stone Face.

But Ernest was kindly, hard working, and neighborly, so the people accepted this habit of his without much comment. They did not know, of course, that the Great Stone Face had become a teacher and guide to him, filling his heart with noble sentiments and with a greater wisdom than could be learned in books.

By this time Mr. Gathergold was dead, and it happened that he had lost a great part of his riches even before his death. With the disappearance of his money, people generally began to admit that he did not resemble the Great Stone Face and that he did not have the character of a great man. So the people ceased to honor him and soon he was forgotten completely. The prediction of the Great Stone Face was still unfulfilled.

It next happened, however, that another man, born in the valley, had left many years ago and had become a soldier. After years of hard fighting, he had advanced to the position of a famous general. His real name was seldom mentioned but he was known in the army as Old Blood and Thunder. This famous general, now old, and tired of the hard life of the army, felt a desire to return to the quiet life of the valley where he had been born. The inhabitants of the valley heard of this desire of the general's and decided to welcome him with a public dinner and a military salute of cannon. It was also said now that the general resembled the Great Stone Face, and an assistant of Old Blood and Thunder, who had passed through the valley, was greatly impressed by the resemblance of the general to the Great Stone Face. His neighbors from his early days and people who had gone to school with him also insisted now that they remembered very well that, as a boy, the general greatly resembled the Great Stone Face.

On the day of the great public dinner, people in the valley stopped work and came from far and near to see the great general who sat at a long table with other important people.

There were several important speeches and each speaker rose to his feet and spoke in praise of the many celebrated events in the life of the great man. Meantime, Ernest could hear the comments of various individuals in the crowd who were comparing the features of the hero with the face on the distant mountainside.

"It is exactly the same face," said one man.

"It is similar in every detail," said another.

"And why not?" asked a third. "The general is the greatest man of this or any other age."

And then all three of the speakers gave a great shout. The excitement spread until the noise could be heard for miles throughout the valley. All these comments and the great enthusiasm of the crowd naturally interested Ernest and he did not question that the great man had come. It is true that Ernest had imagined that the long expected person would be a man of peace, not a man of war, a man who would speak kindly and gently and would do much good throughout the valley. But apparently he had been mistaken.

"The General! The General!" was now the cry. "Quiet! Silence! The general himself is going to make a speech."

The general now rose to his feet to speak to the people and thank them for the demonstration. Ernest could see him at last. There he was, above the crowd, in his military uniform. Was there such a resemblance between him and the Great Stone Face? Ernest saw, instead, a tired and weather-beaten face, full of energy and expressive of a character of iron—but there was missing the gentle wisdom, the deep and tender sympathy of the Great Stone Face.

"No, this is not the man of the tradition," said Ernest to himself as he left the crowd. "And the world must wait even longer for his coming."

As he walked Ernest looked again at the Great Stone Face.

The face was partly covered now by low hanging clouds. But the sun shone through the clouds, and the noble features were still visible. Again the lips of his great friend seemed to move and to say:

"Do not fear, Ernest: Do not fear: Some day he will come."

PART IV

More years passed by—rapidly and quietly. Ernest still lived in the valley and was now a man of middle age. Gradually he had become known among the people. He worked hard and was still the same simple-hearted man that he had always been. But he had thought and felt so much, and he had given so much of his time and thought to good deeds that his wisdom and kindness had gained for him a kind of fame among the people. At the same time he had become a minister, and he went through the valley giving simple sermons to the people. Those who listened to him never suspected that Ernest, their own neighbor and friend, was more than an ordinary man, and Ernest himself did not suspect it, but, when he spoke to the people, noble thoughts, which no other human lips had spoken, came from his mouth.

When the people's minds had had a chance to cool, they were ready to admit that they had made a mistake in imagining that there was a resemblance between the general, Old Blood and Thunder, and the Great Stone Face. But now, again, there were rumors and reports in the newspapers stating that another man had appeared, a great statesman, who greatly resembled the Great Stone Face in every detail. This man also was a native of the valley but had left it many years ago and had entered politics. Instead of the money of the rich man and the sword of the general, this man had only a tongue, — but it was stronger than both together. He was so wonderfully eloquent that his listeners had no choice except to believe him. His tongue was like a magic instrument and he could make his audience do whatever he wished. In truth, he was a wonderful and capable man, and finally he gained great success everywhere throughout the country. He rose from one high office to another until at last he was selected as a candidate for the office of President of the United States.

At this time the candidate decided to visit the valley where he was born in order to shake hands with some of his old friends. Great preparations were naturally made by all the people to receive him. A group of horsemen went to meet him at the boundary of the state and to accompany him along the way. The important people also gathered to greet him. Among these was Ernest. Like the others, Ernest believed that at last the great man of destiny was now going to appear, because Ernest had a hopeful and kind nature, and he was always ready to believe in whatever seemed beautiful and good.

The group of horsemen came down the road. All the important men of the neighborhood were there, military officers in uniform, members of congress, the editors of the important newspapers and others. It was really a brilliant spectacle. There was music and there were flags. On some of the flags there were pictures of the statesman and of the Great Stone Face, facing each other and smiling like two brothers. In these pictures, it must be confessed, the resemblance between the statesman and the Great Stone Face was very clear.

PART V

Meanwhile the people were throwing their hats into the air and shouting. Ernest, too, feeling the same enthusiasm, threw his hat into the air and joined the shouting.

"Hurrah for the Great Man! Hurrah for the Great Man!" But as yet Ernest had not seen him.

Soon, however, a carriage drawn by four white horses appeared. The statesman sat inside, bowing and smiling to the crowd.

Now it must be admitted that at first Ernest did think there was a resemblance between the statesman and the Great Stone Face. There was the same broad forehead, the same strong features. But there was also something lacking. The expression of the face was less kind, less sympathetic. There was not the same noble quality of the eyes. It was as if the statesman, although he had done many wonderful things during his lifetime, had led a life which was vague and empty because no high purpose had ever really inspired him.

Still, Ernest's neighbor pressed him for an answer:

"Confess! Confess! Is he not the exact picture of the Great Stone Face?"

"No," said Ernest, simply. "I see little or no resemblance."

"Then it is too bad for the Great Stone Face because he is really a great man," said the other and immediately began to shout again for the statesman.

Ernest turned away, sad and melancholy. He was sad because once again he had waited for the man who would fulfill the tradition but the man had not come. Through the dust of the procession, however, he could see in the distance the Great Stone Face.

"Here I am, Ernest," the lips seemed to say. "I have waited longer than you have, and am not yet tired. Do not fear. The man will come."

The years passed by.

Ernest grew still older. He was now a man with white hair. But he had not grown old in vain. With his white hair had also come deep wisdom and understanding. He was also quite famous now throughout the valley and even beyond the limits of the valley. College professors and even the active men of the cities came great distances in order to see him and to converse with him; for it was said that this simple man had ideas unlike those of other men, not gained from books but of a higher tone, as if he had been talking with angels as his daily friends. Ernest received all these visitors—statesmen, literary men, professors—with the gentle sincerity that had characterized him since boyhood, and he spoke freely with them of whatever was deep in his heart or in theirs. When they spoke together his face would shine upon them as with a soft evening light. Later, when his guests left and passed through the valley, they often paused and looked up at the Great Stone Face. It seemed to them that they had seen its likeness somewhere in a human face, but they could not remember where.

Meanwhile, during these years, another man, born in the valley, had also become famous. He was a poet. He had spent the greater part of his life in distant cities, but he often returned to the valley to view the mountains and the familiar places of his childhood, which he loved dearly. He often wrote about the valley in his poetry and, more than once, mentioned the Great Stone Face in his inspired writings. His poetry was simple but beautiful, and his talents were so great that whatever he wrote about seemed to the reader to be even more beautiful and real than it appeared in nature.

The verses of this poet found their way to Ernest. Ernest read them after his customary day's work, seated on a bench before his simple home, where so often he had filled his mind with quiet thought while looking at the Great Stone Face. The verses filled his soul with such admiration that he raised his eyes to the Great Stone Face and murmured:

"Oh, great friend! Is not this man worthy to resemble you?"

The face seemed to smile, but answered not a word.

Now it happened that the poet, although he lived in a distant city, had also heard of Ernest and had a great desire to talk with this simple man who, although uneducated, had won fame because of his wisdom and noble thoughts. Therefore, one day the poet came to the valley and, with his suitcase in his hand, approached the house where Ernest lived. Ernest sat before the door with a book in his hand, reading and stopping at times, as was his custom, to look upon the Great Stone Face.

"Good afternon," said the poet, "Can you give a traveler a room for the night?"

"Gladly," said Ernest, "I don't think I have ever seen the Great Stone Face look so kindly upon a stranger."

PART VI

The poet sat down on the bench beside Ernest, and he and Ernest talked together. The poet had talked with many wise and famous men but never before with a man like Ernest, whose thoughts and feelings were so simple yet so noble. Ernest, too, was greatly impressed by the poet, whose speech and conversation were so brilliant that it was a pleasure just to sit and listen to him. The two men, in other words, found very much to admire in each other.

As Ernest listened to the poet, he imagined that the Great Stone Face was leaning forward and also trying to listen.

"Who are you, my very talented friend?" Ernest asked.

The poet placed his finger on the book which Ernest was reading.

"You have read these poems," he said. "Then you know me—for I wrote them."

Again and again Ernest looked carefully into the poet's face and examined his features. He turned toward the Great Stone Face, then back again to his guest. Finally he shook his head in sadness.

"Why are you sad?" asked the poet.

"Because all through my life I have waited for the fulfillment of a prediction, and, when I read these poems, I hoped that the prediction might be fulfilled in you."

"You hoped to find in me the likeness of the Great Stone Face. And you are sad because like Mr. Gathergold, Old Blood and Thunder, and the others, I do not resemble the Great Stone Face. No, it is unfortunate but I am not worthy to resemble that majestic image."

"And why?" asked Ernest. He pointed to the book of poems. "Are these thoughts not divine?"

"Perhaps they have a touch of divinity but that is all. And my life has not corresponded always with my thoughts. I have had great dreams but they have only been dreams—and I have done nothing except write. No, I am afraid I am not a great man."

The poet spoke quietly, and his eyes were sad. Sad, also, were the eyes of Ernest.

In the early evening, as was his custom, Ernest went to speak to a group of the neighboring inhabitants in the open air. He and the poet, arm in arm, still talking as they walked along, proceeded to the place, which was situated some distance away at the foot of a high mountain. The place was surrounded by a group of high trees and was a kind of natural, outdoor meeting place.

There was a large stone at the back which served as a platform or pulpit. Ernest mounted this pulpit and began to speak, giving to the people what was in his heart and mind. His words had power because they corresponded with his thoughts and with his deeds. They had reality because they harmonized with the daily life which he had always lived. The poet, as he listened, felt that the being and character of Ernest were a more noble kind of poetry than anything he had ever written. As he looked at Ernest he said to himself that Ernest's face was truly that of a prophet and a great man. In the distance, but easily to be seen in the golden light of the setting sun, was also the Great Stone Face with the same nobility of expression that was visible in Ernest's face.

At that moment, in sympathy with a thought which he was about to express, the face of Ernest assumed such an expression of greatness and nobility that the poet, by an irresistible impulse, threw up his hands and shouted:

"Look! Look! Ernest himself is the likeness of the Great Stone Face."

Then all the people looked and saw that what the deep-sighted poet said was true. The prediction was fulfilled at last. But Ernest, having finished what he had to say, took the poet's arm and walked humbly toward his home, still hoping that some wiser and better man than he would later appear, resembling more exactly the Great Stone Face.

Exercises Based on

THE GREAT STONE FACE

PART I

A. Answer These Questions:

1. What two persons sit at the door of their home talking of the Great Stone Face, when this story opens? 2. Was it easy or difficult to see the Great Stone Face from where they sat? 3. Did many or few people live in this particular valley? 4. Were the inhabitants all of the same social class or were some of them poor and others wealthy? 5. Were all the inhabitants familiar or unfamiliar with the Great Stone Face? 6. Did all of the inhabitants see the Great Stone Face equally well or could some distinguish its features more easily than others?

7. Was the Great Stone Face a work of nature or an artificial work made by man? 8. Did the Great Stone Face have all the features of a human face or only a few of the features? 9. What do we mean when we say, speaking of a person, that he or she has good features? 10. Was it easier to distinguish the features of the Great Stone Face from a distance or from a position very close? 11. Were the features of the face noble and kind or ugly and unpleasant? 12. Did the people of the valley think that the Great Stone Face was a good influence or a bad influence upon their lives? 13. What tradition existed in the valley regarding the Great Stone Face? 14. Had this tradition existed for many years or for a few years? 15. Was Ernest interested or uninterested in his mother's story of the Great Stone Face?

B. Vocabulary Drill. Choose The Correct Form:

1. A *valley* usually lies between (two rivers, two hills or mountains, two small villages).

2. Give the corresponding noun form of these adjectives: deep, wide, high, familiar, poor, long, kind, noble.

3. The word *height* is pronounced to rhyme with (eight, hit, bite, caught).

4. *Thunder* is usually accompanied by (sunshine, loud cries, lightning, snow).

5. *Gigantic* means (clever, small, very large, fertile).

6. Give the plural form of these nouns: child, man, valley, city, country, church, wish, phenomenon, story, foot, woman.

7. A synonym for *immense* is (exact, huge, noble, thoughtful).

8. Distinguish in use between *raise* and *rise*. Use each correctly in a sentence.

9. Give the opposites of these words by adding the necessary prefix: kind, familiar, able, possible, appear, inhabited, comfortable, natural, fortunate, educated, regular, real, patient.

10. How many syllables does each of these words contain and on which syllable does the accent fall: influence, tradition, previously, looked, believed, appeared, inhabitant, familiar, talked?

C. Use These In Sentences:

to talk about, in other words, to be familiar with, to grow up, to look at, to throw together, according to, to believe in, to wait for, to sit at.

PART II

A. Answer These Questions:

1. Was Ernest a good boy or a bad boy? 2. Did he spend much time or little time helping his mother? 3. Did he grow up to be a strong young man or a weak young man? 4. Did Ernest go to school or did he have only the Great Stone Face as a teacher? 5. Was Ernest an intelligent or an unintelligent young man? 6. What rumor concerning a prediction connected with the Great Stone Face went around the valley at this time? 7. Was the great man who was expected at this time a business man or a professional man? 8. Was he a very rich man or a very poor man? 9. Why did Mr. Gathergold decide at last to return to the valley? 10. Did Mr. Gathergold want to build a modest home or an impressive mansion? 11. Was the exterior of the house to be made of marble or of wood? 12. Was Ernest very anxious to see the great man or was he indifferent to his coming? 13. Was Mr. Gathergold, when he arrived, young and handsome or old and wrinkled? 14. Did Ernest see much resemblance or little resemblance between Mr. Gathergold and the Great Stone Face? 15. What encouraging words, however, did the Great Stone Face seem to speak to Ernest as he looked toward it?

B. Vocabulary Drill. Choose The Correct Form:

1. A common synonym for *assist* is (need, repay, entertain, help).
2. If a person is *sun-burned,* this means that he is (happy, a little crazy, dizzy from the heat, well tanned).
3. Give the corresponding noun form of these adjectives: intelligent, kind, wealthy, distant, original, long, deep, important.
4. A person whose skin is *wrinkled* is generally (very young, deeply worried, very old, very rich).
5. *Enormous* means (wealthy, too small, intelligent, very large).
6. A synonym for *at last* is (surely, finally, rarely, recently).
7. Give the opposites of these words: exterior, old, inside, wrinkled, thin, sharp, true, last, arrive, arrival, long, end, rich.
8. A *pillar* is a (kind of cushion, tall post, servant, carriage).
9. Use each of these words in a sentence, once as a noun and once as a verb: doubt, return, cry, work, fear, turn, help, influence, smile.

10. In which of these words is the letter *s* pronounced like *s* and in which is it pronounced like *z*: was, case, resemble, perhaps, always, noise, lose, loose, lips, child's, position, raise, rise.

C. Use These In Sentences:

to grow up, to look at, in return, to be supposed to, to be born, at least, to go into business, according to, to wait for, to look like.

PART III

A. Answer These Questions:

1. Did Ernest attract little or much attention in the valley? 2. Was he an unpleasant young man or was he kindly? 3. Was he lazy or hard working? 4. By the time of his death had Mr. Gathergold gained more wealth or had he lost a large part of his riches? 5. Did the people continue to honor Mr. Gathergold or was he soon forgotten? 6. Was the prediction of the Great Stone Face thus fulfilled or was it still unfulfilled? 7. What second famous man, born in the valley, now decided to return? 8. Was this man a famous diplomat or a famous soldier? 9. In what way did the people of the valley decide to welcome him? 10. Was there supposed to be little or much resemblance between the general and the Great Stone Face? 11. Was there little or much enthusiasm for the general? 12. Was Ernest again interested or uninterested in seeing the great man? 13. When Ernest at last saw the general, did he notice little or much resemblance with the Great Stone Face? 14. In what way did the face of the general differ in expression from the Great Stone Face? 15. What words, again, did the Great Stone Face seem to speak to Ernest as he now looked toward it?

B. Vocabulary Drill. Choose The Correct Form:

1. *Neighborly* means (nearby, friendly and helpful, critical, angry).

2. His day's work is *over* means that his day's work is (difficult, finished, never done, interesting).

3 The word *guide* is pronounced to rhyme with (need, laid, lied, tight).

4. Give the corresponding adjective form of these nouns: energy, sympathy, wisdom, similarity, enthusiasm.

5. The opposite of *admit* is (deceive, deny, decide, discover).

6. A synonym for *seldom* is (frequently, never, occasionally, rarely).

7. To *cease* to do something is to (want to do it, hope to do it, stop doing it, avoid doing it).

8. He could hear their *comments* means that he could hear their (cries, criticism, speeches, remarks).

9. Give the corresponding noun form of these verbs: compare, resemble, impress, sympathize, predict, decide, attract.

10. A common synonym for *mistaken* is (confused, recent, wrong, distant).

C. Use These In Sentences:

to go on, to attract attention, to be over, by this time, to pass through, to be impressed by, as a boy, from far and near.

PART IV

A. Answer These Questions:

1. As the years passed by did Ernest continue to live in the valley or did he move elsewhere? 2. Did he remain unknown or did he gradually gain a kind of fame? 3. Had he become a minister or a teacher? 4. Did Ernest go through the valley giving elaborate sermons or very simple sermons? 5. Did the people finally admit that they had made a mistake in imagining that there was a resemblance between the general and the Great Stone face? 6. What new rumors and reports now appeared in the newspapers and throughout the valley? 7. Was this new man a soldier or a politician? 8. Did he have great ability or little ability as a public speaker? 9. Was he finally selected as a candidate for senator or as a candidate for President? 10. Which is the more important position, senator or President of the United States? 11. Which is the more important position, senator or congressman (member of the House of Representatives)? 12. How many senators are there in the Senate of the United States? 13. Approximately how many congressmen are there in the House of Representatives? 14.

When the great statesman decided to visit the valley, what preparations were made to meet him? 15. Whose pictures appeared on the flags that were carried in the procession?

B. Vocabulary Drill. Choose The Correct Form:

1. *Gradually* means (rapidly, now and then, soon, little by little).

2. Distinguish between *kind* used as an adjective and *kind* used as a noun.

3. Give the corresponding noun form of these adjectives: wise, kind, famous, successful, high, important, beautiful, brilliant, strong.

4. Distinguish in meaning between the words *statesman* and *politician.*

5. The word *sword* is pronounced to rhyme with (word, swore, toured, poured).

6. The word *tongue* is pronounced to rhyme with (song, sung, wrong, strong).

7. A common synonym for *select* is (accompany, appear, admit, choose).

8. Give the corresponding noun form of these verbs: select, believe, confess, succeed, resemble, enter, suspect, admit.

9. Use these four words in sentences, showing clearly the difference in meaning: neighbor, neighborly, neighboring, neighborhood.

10. Which of these past tense forms are pronounced as words of one syllable and which are pronounced as words of two syllables: counted, wanted, passed, lived, talked, gained, needed, seemed.

C. Use These In Sentences:

to pass by, to become known, to listen to, in truth, in order to, to shake hands, along the way, to believe in, to face each other.

PART V

A. Answer These Questions:

1. At first, did Ernest see a resemblance or a lack of resemblance between the statesman and the Great Stone Face? 2. In what way,

however, was the expression of the two faces different? 3. Which face was lacking in nobility of expression? 4. What did the lips of the Great Stone Face again seem to say to him? 5. As he grew older did Ernest gain or lose in wisdom and understanding? 6. Was he still unknown or had he become quite famous? 7. Why did college professors and other important men come great distances in order to see him and converse with him? 8. Was Ernest greatly impressed by all this attention or did he receive these people with his usual simplicity and sincerity? 9. What other man, born in the valley, had become famous during these years? 10. Did this man seldom or often write about the valley in his poetry? 11. Did Ernest find the poetry of this man inspiring or uninspiring? 12. Had the poet also heard of Ernest or was Ernest completely unknown to him? 13. What famous American poets can you name? 14. Which do you enjoy more, poetry or prose? 15. What are the technical differences between poetry and prose?

B. Vocabulary Drill. Choose The Correct Form:

1. Give the opposites of these words: empty, high, broad, many, much, sad, older, deep, active, simple, soft, often, familiar, beautiful.

2. Something *lacking* means something (new, necessary, added, missing).

3. To do something *in vain* means to do it (thoroughly, in time, uselessly or without result, steadily).

4. The word *pause* is pronounced to rhyme with (knows, sauce, laws, crawls).

5. A common synonym for *melancholy* is (happy, inspired, sad, crazy).

6. Give the corresponding noun form of these adjectives: sincere, kind, noble, sympathetic, empty, sad, distant, deep, soft, high, familiar, real, simple, enthusiastic.

7. To *murmur* is to (shout, cry bitterly, sing sweetly, speak in a very low voice).

8. Another name for *suitcase* is (pocketbook, portfolio, copybook, traveling bag).

9. Which of these is part of the face (neck, knee, forehead, elbow)?

10. Give sentences with these three words, making clear the differences in meaning: poem, poet, poetry.

C. Use These In Sentences:

to turn away, to wait for, in the distance, in vain, to look up at, more than once, to hear of, to win fame, at times.

PART VI

A. Answer These Questions:

1. Was Ernest impressed or unimpressed in his conversation with the poet? 2. Did the two men find much or little to admire in each other? 3. Who was the author of the book Ernest was reading at this time? 4. Why was Ernest disappointed after examining carefully the face of the poet? 5. Did the face of the poet bear little or much resemblance to the Great Stone Face? 6. Had a great man who resembled the Great Stone Face yet appeared or was the prediction still unfulfilled? 7. Where did Ernest go to speak one evening? 8. Did he go alone or did the poet accompany him? 9. Did the poet feel that the expression in Ernest's face was the same as the expression of the Great Stone Face or different from it? 10. What did the poet suddenly shout, throwing up his hands? 11. What prediction had thus been finally fulfilled? 12. Did Ernest himself believe that he resembled the Great Stone Face or did he hope that some wiser and better man would still appear? 13. Did he walk proudly toward his home or did he walk humbly as usual? 14. Did Ernest always speak in an artificial or in a natural manner? 15. Was the place where Ernest had spoken located indoors or outdoors?

B. Vocabulary Drill. Choose The Correct Form:

1. A *bench* is (a large stone, a long, low seat, an outdoor meeting place, a kind of poetry).

2. Pick out the silent letters in these words: listen, whistle, talk, character, knife, pneumonia, whole, sword, neighbor.

3. Distinguish in meaning between *mind* used as a verb and *mind* used as a noun.

4. Give the opposites of these words: outdoor, careful, outside, quiet, sad, natural, early, easily, visible, true.

5. The word *wise* is pronounced to rhyme with (price, seize, size, lace).

6. *Pulpits* are generally used only by (judges, choir boys, priests or ministers, policemen).

7. *Truly great* means (rather great, really great, seldom great, not at all great).

8. How many syllables does each of the following words contain and on which syllable does the accent fall: harmonize, walked, fulfilled, talked, finished, resembled, sympathy, irresistible, placed?

9. Distinguish in meaning between *lean* used as an adjective and *lean* used as a verb.

10. Which one of these words is not spelled correctly: easily, inhabitant, surrounded, neighborhood, image, harmonize?

C. Use These In Sentences:

to lean forward, to shake one's head, arm in arm, to serve as, some distance away, to correspond with, to harmonize with, to say to oneself, in the distance.

RIP VAN WINKLE

Washington Irving

PART I

Anyone who has made a voyage up the Hudson River remembers the Catskill Mountains. They rise to great height and make a deep impression upon all who look upon them. Every change of season, every change of weather, and every hour of the day makes some change in the magical colors and shapes of these mountains, and all the good wives from far and near thus consider them perfect barometers and are able to look at them and predict what the weather will be.

At the foot of the mountains the traveler may see smoke rising slowly from a small village whose roofs shine among the trees. It is a very old village, which was founded by the Dutch, and some of the houses of the first settlers were still standing until a few years ago.

In this village and in one of these very houses (which, to tell the exact truth, was very old and weather-beaten) there lived many years ago, while the country was still a province of Great Britain, a simple, good-natured fellow named Rip Van Winkle. Besides being a good-natured man, Rip Van Winkle was a kind neighbor and a meek, obedient husband. He was meek because his wife was very severe with him and often scolded him and shouted at him, making his life difficult. But he was very popular with everyone else, possibly because of his meekness. He was a great favorite among all the good wives of the village, who, as usual in such cases, took his side in all the family disputes, and, when they talked these matters over at night, always placed the blame on Mrs. Van Winkle. The children of the village, too, would shout with joy whenever he approached. He assisted them in all their sports, made their playthings, and taught them how to play various games. He also told the children long stories of Indians and of strange lands and strange peoples. Wherever he went, children followed him, climbed upon his back, and played friendly tricks on him. Everyone knew him and loved him. Not a dog in the village barked at him.

The great flaw in Rip's character was a strong aversion for all kinds of work. He could sit all day long and fish, without catching anything and he would never complain. With a gun on his shoulder, he could walk for hours through the woods, up hill and down hill, to shoot only a few squirrels. He was the most important person at all the country parties and dances. He was always ready to help a neighbor in the hardest kind of work. But as to doing family duty and keeping his own farm in order, he found this impossible. In a word, he was ready to attend to everybody's business except his own.

PART II

He insisted that it was useless to work on his own farm. He said it was the worst piece of land in the whole country. Everything about it went wrong. His fences were always falling down, and his cow always got lost or escaped into the vegetable garden. Nothing would grow in his fields, and it always rained when he wanted to do some outdoor work. He had inherited a beautiful, big farm from his father, but it grew smaller and smaller under Rip's care until there was nothing left but a small garden where a little corn and potatoes grew. Rip's little farm was in the worst condition of any farm in the neighborhood.

Rip's children, too, looked as wild and poorly dressed as if they belonged to nobody. His son, also called Rip, who looked just like him, had the same habits as his father. He ran at his mother's heels dressed in a pair of his father's old trousers, which he had much trouble to hold up with one hand.

Rip Van Winkle, however, was one of those happy, simple people who take the world easy. He would eat white bread or brown bread, whichever he could get with the least thought or trouble. He would rather starve on one cent than work for five dollars. The only thing that disturbed his happiness, however, was his wife who constantly scolded him for his laziness and carelessness. He was bringing ruin on the family, she said. Morning, noon and night her tongue was going continuously, and everything Rip did or said produced additional scolding on his wife's part. Rip's only friend at home at such times was his dog, Wolf, and the poor dog was almost as miserable as Rip himself, for Mrs. Van Winkle also scolded Wolf and said that Rip and he were companions in laziness. Wolf was a courageous animal, but what animal can stand up against the constant scolding of a woman? When Wolf entered the house, his tail dropped between his legs and stayed there, and he would fly from the house if Mrs. Van Winkle picked up a broom or some similar object.

Times grew worse and worse with Rip Van Winkle as years of married life went on. The character of his wife grew less and less sweet, and, of course, a sharp tongue only grows sharper with constant use. For a long time Rip used to find comfort by going to the village inn where a group of the village men sat and smoked all day and discussed the news of the day. Among this group were Mr. Von Bummel, the village schoolmaster, who knew every word in the dictionary, and Mr. Nicholas Vedder, one of the oldest men in the village and the owner of the inn. But even this group of important personages offered little refuge to Rip, for his wife often interrupted the quiet of the group and began to scold all of them for their laziness. Even that great person, Nicholas Vedder himself, was not safe from the awful criticism of Rip's scolding wife.

Finally, the only way in which Rip could escape both from his farm and from the constant scolding of his wife was to take his gun and dog and go off into the woods. There he would sit down at the foot of a tree and give part of his lunch to Wolf. He sympathized deeply with Wolf and often said: "Poor Wolf, your mistress treats you like a dog. But never mind! While I live you will always have a friend to support you!" Wolf would look affectionately into his master's eyes, and I believe he understood with all his heart.

PART III

One fine autumn day Rip climbed to one of the highest parts of the Catskill Mountains. He was doing what he liked to do—hunting squirrels—and the quiet woods echoed and re-echoed with the sound of his gun. Out of breath and tired, he lay down on the green grass at the top of a hill. From here he looked out over all the lower country for many miles. He saw the noble Hudson River far, far below him, moving slowly along. He looked down the other side into a deep valley. The bottom of the valley was filled with rocks which had fallen from the mountains above. For some time Rip lay there half asleep. Evening was approaching and the mountains began to throw their long, blue shadows over the valley. Rip saw that it would be dark long before he reached the valley, and he sighed deeply when he thought about Mrs. Van Winkle.

He started to go down the valley when he heard a voice calling, "Rip Van Winkle! Rip Van Winkle!" He looked around but could see nothing except a lonely bird flying across the mountains. He thought that he had been mistaken and began again to descend when he heard the same voice: "Rip Van Winkle! Rip Van Winkle!" At the same time Wolf gave a low bark and came close to his master's side. Rip now began to feel a little afraid. He looked anxiously into the valley and then saw a strange little man slowly climbing up the mountain side and carrying something heavy on his back. Rip was surprised to see anyone in this lonely place but he thought it was possibly one of his neighbors in need of some help, so he hurried down to meet him.

As he came nearer, he was greatly surprised at the strangeness of the man's appearance. The man was a short, square-built old fellow, with thick hair and a beard. He was dressed in the old Dutch fashion. He wore a very short coat and several pairs of trousers. The outer trousers were very large and were decorated with rows of buttons down the sides. This strange little man carried on his back a small barrel that seemed full of liquor, and he motioned for Rip to come and help him. Rip was rather afraid, but as usual he was always ready to assist anyone. He helped the man and together they proceeded up the mountain. They proceeded some distance along what seemed to be the dry bed of a former mountain stream. Occasionally Rip heard what sounded like distant thunder although the skies were clear and there were no signs of storms. These sounds seemed to come from the direction in which they were walking. They passed around the side of the mountain and thus came at last to a level place that resembled a small amphitheater, surrounded by tall trees. All this time Rip and his companion had climbed the mountain in silence. Rip wondered why this stranger was carrying a small barrel of liquor up this wild mountain but there was something so strange about the unknown man that Rip was deeply impressed and was afraid to speak to him.

When they entered the amphitheatre Rip saw other strange things. In the center was a group of unusual looking men playing an old Dutch game called ninepins, in which they rolled large balls at small sticks placed upon the ground. All the men were dressed in very strange costumes, similar to the costume of Rip's companion. Their faces too were not quite normal. One had a large beard, a broad face, and small eyes like those of a pig. The face of another was almost entirely nose, and he wore a round, white hat with a red feather in it. They all had beards of various shapes and colors. There was one who seemed to be the commander. He was a fat old gentleman with a weather-beaten face. He wore a short coat, broad belt, high hat with a feather in it, red stockings, and high heeled shoes. These men made Rip think of the men in a very old Dutch painting, brought from Holland, that he had once seen.

PART IV

Rip thought that it was very strange that while these men were amusing themselves, they all had such serious faces and remained so mysteriously silent. Nothing interrupted the quiet except the noise of the balls which echoed along the mountains like thunder and which was the noise which Rip had heard as they came up the mountain.

When Rip and his companion came near, the men stopped playing and stood looking at Rip. They looked at him in such a strange manner and with such strange, deathly faces that Rip's heart turned within him and his knees began to knock together. His companion now emptied the liquor into large bottles and made signs to Rip to wait a moment. Rip obeyed with fear. The strange men drank the liquor in deep silence, and then they returned to their game.

Little by little Rip's fears grew less. He even dared, when no one was looking to taste the liquor, which was excellent Holland gin. Rip was naturally a thirsty soul, and he soon took another drink. One taste made him want another. He repeated his drinks so often that his eyes swam in his head, his head became heavy, and he fell into a deep sleep.

When he woke up he found himself back on the green grass from where he had first seen the old man coming towards him up the mountain. He rubbed his eyes—it was a bright, sunny morning. The birds were singing in the trees. "Surely," thought Rip, "I have not slept here all night." He thought of what had happened before he fell asleep. He remembered the strange man with the small barrel of liquor on his back. He remembered the sad group of men playing ninepins. "Oh, that liquor! That terrible liquor," thought Rip. "What excuse shall I make to my wife?"

He looked around for his gun, but he found only an old rusty gun lying beside him. He thought that the strange men whom he had met had played a trick on him. They had given him liquor and then stolen his gun. Wolf, too, had disappeared, but Wolf possibly had gone after a squirrel. Rip whistled for his dog and shouted his name. The echoes repeated his whistle and shout, but no dog came.

He decided to go where he had been last evening, and if he found any of the men he would demand his dog and gun. As he got up to walk, however, he found that his legs and his whole body were stiff.

"These mountain beds do not agree with me," thought Rip. With great difficulty he climbed the mountain along the route that he and his companion had taken the night before. To his great surprise he found a stream of water now running where last night there had only been the dry bed. He finally came to the amphitheatre but it was filled now with trees and great stones. He again called and whistled for his dog, but there was no answer. It was now almost noon and he was very hungry. He did not wish to lose his dog and gun and he was afraid to meet his wife, but he also did not want to die of hunger. He shook his head, put his rusty gun on his shoulder, and, with a heart full of trouble, he started down the mountain.

As he approached the village, he met a number of people whom he did not know. This surprised him, for he thought he knew everyone in the country around. The people's clothes were different from those to which he was accustomed. They all looked at him in a very strange way. They did this so often that finally Rip passed his hand over his face to find out what was wrong and discovered, to his surprise, that his beard had grown a foot long.

PART V

He now came to the edge of the village. A crowd of strange children ran after him, shouting and pointing at his gray beard. The dogs, too, which he did not recognize, barked at him as he passed. The village itself was changed; it was larger and there were more people. There were houses which he had never seen before and the houses which he had known so well had disappeared. Rip couldn't believe his eyes. Surely this was his native village, which he had left only the day before. There stood the Catskill Mountains—there was the beautiful Hudson River. Rip was badly confused. "That bottle of liquor last night," he thought, "has mixed up my poor head badly."

At last with great difficulty, Rip found the way to his own house, expecting every minute to hear the sharp voice of Mrs. Van Winkle. He found the house, but the roof had fallen in and the windows and doors were broken. The house was also empty and abandoned. He went in and called loudly for his wife and children; the lonely rooms rang for a moment with his voice, and then all was silence.

Next he hurried toward the old village inn—but that was gone. In its place was a large building with big windows, and over the door a sign, "The Union Hotel". Instead of the great tree, under which Rip and his friends used to sit and smoke, there was now a tall pole with a strange looking flag of stars and stripes. There was also a crowd of people around the door, but Rip did not recognize any of them. The very character of the people seemed to have changed. They were all busy and hurrying about instead of quietly sitting and smoking long Dutch pipes. He looked for Nicholas Vedder and for Von Bummel, the schoolmaster, but they were not there.

Rip Van Winkle, with his long beard, his rusty gun, his old clothes, and so many children at his heels soon attracted the attention of the people at the door of the inn. They crowded around him and looked at him from head to foot with great curiosity. They began to ask questions about politics, and one man asked him on which side he was going to vote in the elections. Rip could not understand these questions.

"But what has brought you to the election with a gun on

your shoulder and a crowd of people at your heels?" asked a second man in a severe tone.

"I am a poor, quiet man—and a native of this place," explained Rip.

"But where did you come from and what do you want?"

Rip assured them that he was simply looking for some of his neighbors who always used to sit on the bench in front of the inn.

Someone said: "Well, who are they? Name them."

Rip thought a moment and asked, "Where's Nicholas Vedder?"

There was a silence in the crowd and no one seemed to recognize the name. Then an old man in a thin voice replied, "Nicholas Vedder? Oh, he has been dead and buried some eighteen years."

"Where's Brom Dutcher?" asked Rip.

"Oh, he went off to the army in the beginning of the war. Some say he was killed—others say he was drowned—but he never came back again."

"Where's Von Bummel, the schoolmaster?"

"He went off to the war too, was a great general, and is now in congress."

PART VI

Rip's heart died within him when he heard of these sad changes in his home and friends. He was alone in the world. Also, he was confused by the fact that Nichols Vedder had been dead for eighteen years. Also, what army and what war were they talking about? What did they mean by "congress"? But Rip had no courage to ask for any more friends, and he cried out at last in despair.

"But does nobody here know Rip Van Winkle?"

"Oh, Rip Van Winkle," said two or three. "That's Rip Van Winkle over there, standing against that tree."

Rip looked and saw an exact image of himself as he was when he went up the mountain, apparently as lazy and certainly as poorly dressed. Poor Rip was now completely confused. He doubted his own identity. Was he himself or was he another man? Suddenly someone asked him who he really was and what his name was.

"God knows," replied Rip. "I'm not myself. I'm somebody else. That's me over there. No, it's somebody else in my shoes. I was myself last night but I fell asleep on the mountain, and they have changed my gun and taken my dog. Everything is changed, and I'm changed, and I can't tell who I really am."

The people began to exchange glances with one another as if to say that they thought the poor old fellow was crazy. At this moment a good looking young woman pushed her way through the crowd in order to get a look at the old man. She had a child in her arms who became frightened when he saw Rip and began to cry. "Quiet, Rip," the young woman said to the child, "Don't cry. The old man won't hurt you." The name of the child, the manner of the mother, the tone of her voice awakened memories in Rip's mind.

"What is your name, my good woman?" he asked.

"Judith Gardinier."

"And what was your father's name?"

"Oh, poor man, his name was Rip Van Winkle, but he went away from home twenty years ago with his gun, and no one has seen him since. His dog came home without him, but I don't know whether he shot himself or was captured by the Indians. Nobody knows. I was only a little girl when he went away."

Rip had only one more question to ask, and he asked it with a trembling voice.

"Where's your mother?"

"Oh," said the young woman, "My mother died a short time ago. She became so angry one day that she broke a blood-vessel."

PART VII

There was some comfort at least for Rip in this news of his wife. The old man could control himself no longer. He caught his daughter and her child in his arms. "I am your father!" he cried, "I was young Rip Van Winkle once—I am old Rip Van Winkle now. Does nobody here know poor Rip Van Winkle?"

All stood surprised, until an old woman, coming out of the crowd, put her hand to her forehead, and looking closely into his face for a moment, said, "Yes, it is Rip Van Winkle. Welcome home again, old neighbor. Where have you been these twenty years?"

Rip soon told his story, for the twenty years seemed to him to be only one night. The people could hardly believe him and many thought he was crazy. They finally decided to let old Peter Vanderdonk decide whether Rip was telling the truth or not. Old Peter, who was slowly coming up the road, was the oldest inhabitant of the village and he remembered all of the history and the traditions of the neighborhood. He recognized Rip at once and supported his story in a most satisfactory way. He assured the people that the Catskill mountains had always been inhabited by strange little men. Old Peter said that his own father had once seen a group of them playing ninepins at one time, and that he himself had heard, one summer afternoon, the sound of their playing which seemed like the noise of distant thunder.

To make a long story short, Rip's daughter finally took him home with her and there he continued to live for some years. She had a comfortable little home and a pleasant husband. Rip remembered the husband as one of the small boys who used to climb upon his back.

Rip soon took up his old walks and old habits. He found a few of his old friends but they were all now very old. Once more he sat on the bench at the inn, but it was a long time before he could understand the strange events that had taken place during his long sleep. There had been a Revolutionary War with England and now he was a free citizen of the United States. But Rip was little interested in matters of government. The only government which he had known for years was the strict government of his wife, and now he was happy to have escaped her domination.

Rip used to tell his story to every stranger that arrived at the hotel. At first, he used to vary on some points but finally it became the exact story which has been told here. Every man, woman, and child in the neighborhood knew it by heart. Some people doubted the truth of the story, but all the old Dutch inhabitants believed it entirely. Even to this day when they hear a thunderstorm in the Catskills they say that the strange little men are playing a game of ninepins; and it is a common wish of all the husbands of the neighborhood, when they have trouble with their wives, that they might have a quieting drink of liquor out of old Rip Van Winkle's bottle.

Exercises Based on

RIP VAN WINKLE

PART I

A. Answer These Questions:

1. Are the Catskill Mountains located near the Hudson River or the Mississippi River? 2. Is the Hudson River larger or smaller than the

Mississippi River? 3. Which is the largest river in the United States? 4. Near what large city does the Hudson River flow? 5. Are the Catskill Mountains high and impressive looking or small and unimpressive? 6. How are the good wives of the district able to predict the weather by looking at these mountains? 7. By what people was the village mentioned in this story founded? 8. By what people was the city of New York founded? 9. What is the name of the principal character of this story? 10. Was Rip Van Winkle a good natured fellow or an unpleasant fellow? 11. Was he a kind neighbor or a selfish neighbor? 12. Which do you prefer, kind people or selfish people? 13. What is the noun form of the word *kind?* Of the word *selfish?* 14. Was Rip's wife very gentle or very severe with him? 15. Did she often praise him or often scold him? 16. Was Rip popular or unpopular with everyone in the village? 17. Whose side did the women of the village take in Rip's family disputes, Rip's side or the side of his wife? 18. In what ways did Rip help the children of the village? 19. What was the one great weakness of Rip's character? 20. What were some of the things which Rip preferred to do rather than to work?

B. Vocabulary Drill. Choose The Correct Form:

1. A *voyage* is a (wide river, high mountain, trip, change of season).
2. *Barometers* are used to show the (temperature, direction of the wind, atmospheric pressure).
3. It was *founded* means it was (situated, found and returned, established, situated).
4. Give sentences showing the difference in use between *because* (the conjunction) and *because of* (the preposition).
5. To *talk something over* is to (repeat it several times, admit it, deny it, discuss it).
6. A *dispute* is a (friendly meeting, small village, argument or quarrel, court trial).
7. Distinguish in meaning between *bark* used as a verb and *bark* used as a noun.
8. A *flaw* is a (small animal, insect, defect, kind of plaything).
9. The word *squirrel* is pronounced to rhyme with (trial, peel, barrel, pearl).

10. *Somewhat difficult means* (very difficult, never difficult, rather difficult, not at all difficult).

C. Use These In Sentences:

from far and near, to tell the truth, to shout at, somewhat difficult, in any case, because of, as usual, to talk something over, to play tricks on.

PART II

A. Answer These Questions:

1. Did Rip claim that he had the best or the worst piece of land in the whole country? 2. Were his fences always in good or bad condition? 3. Did the farm which he had inherited from his father grow bigger or smaller under Rip's care? 4. Were Rip's children always well dressed or poorly dressed? 5. Did Rip's son bear little or much resemblance to his father in appearance and in habits? 6. What is the noun form of the verb *inherit?* 7. Was Rip a very serious or a very easy-going fellow? 8. Who was the only person who disturbed Rip's happiness? 9. When Rip's dog, Wolf, entered the house, why did his tail drop between his legs? 10. What would Wolf do whenever Rip's wife picked up a broom? 11. When driven from home by his wife's scolding, would Rip go to work on his farm or would he go to the village inn? 12. Which character do you find more likeable, Rip or his wife? 13. Did Rip's wife scold him continuously or only occasionally? 14. Did the character of Rip's wife grow less pleasant or more pleasant as time went on? 15. Do you think Rip's wife was justified or not in her attitude toward her husband?

B. Vocabulary Drill. Choose The Correct Form:

1. To *rip* something is to (repair it, claim it, need it, tear it).

2. There was nothing *left* means that there was nothing (new, interesting, remaining, needed).

3. To run *at someone's heels* is to run (alongside him, far behind him, just behind him, in front of him).

4. He *would rather starve* means that he (often starved, used to starve, seldom starved, preferred to starve).

5. A synonym for *constantly* is (rarely, continuously, easily, with difficulty).

6. Give the corresponding noun form of these adjectives: lazy, careless, courageous, similar, beautiful, happy, sweet, important, safe, deep, affectionate.

7. A common synonym for *ruin* is (comfort, a sharp tongue, destruction, constant scolding).

8. A common synonym for *courageous* is (lazy, careless, brave, cowardly).

9. Which of these can we use to *sweep* out a room (a hammer, a ruler, a broom, a shotgun)?

10. An *inn* is a (small village, small hotel, vegetable garden, scolding wife).

C. Use These In Sentences:

to go wrong, to fall down, to get lost, as if, to be dressed in, to take things easy, to pick up, to go on, of course, used to.

PART III

A. Answer These Questions:

1. Where did Rip Van Winkle climb one fine autumn day? 2. Was he hunting bears or squirrels? 3. Is a squirrel a large animal or a small animal? 4. Is a squirrel a wild animal or a domestic animal? 5. For what are the skins of squirrels sometimes used? 6. When Rip started to go down the valley, whom did he hear calling him? 7. Was the strange man whom he saw very small or very large? 8. Was he carrying something in his hand or on his back? 9. Was the man dressed in modern fashion or in old Dutch fashion? 10. What was he carrying on his back? 11. Did Rip and the man talk much together as they walked or did they both remain silent? 12. As they entered the amphitheatre, what strange sight did Rip see? 13. What game were the strange men playing? 14. Were the men whom Rip saw very strange looking or normal looking people? 15. Were the men beardless or did they all have beards of various shapes and colors?

B. Vocabulary Drill. Choose The Correct Form:

1. A common synonym for *autumn* is (spring, change of season, fall, winter).

2. Give sentences with these: out of breath, out of sight, out of hearing, out of order, out of date.

3. Generally, a person *sighs* only when he is (happy, hungry, drunk, sad).

4. A common synonym for *lonely* is (dizzy, lonesome, tired, discouraged).

5. The word *hurried* is pronounced to rhyme with (married, feared, worried, cared).

6. The word *beard* is pronounced to rhyme with (cared, bored, bird, feared).

7. Give the corresponding noun form of these adjectives: lonely, anxious, dark, strange, possible, dry, distant, clear, deep, high, silent, similar.

8. An old Dutch *fashion* means an old Dutch (game, style, painting, dish).

9. A common conversational equivalent of *occasionally* is (right away, now and then, just now, after awhile).

10. Use each of these words in sentences, once as a noun and once as a verb: dress, roll, face, place, look, sound, sign, walk, surprise, sigh, call.

C. Use These In Sentences:

out of breath, to lie down, for some time, to look around, to be mistaken, to feel afraid, to climb up, as usual, at last, in silence.

PART IV

A. Answer These Questions:

1. Did the strange men playing the game of ninepins appear happy in their game or did they all play with very serious faces? 2. Did they shout and laugh or did they remain mysteriously silent? 3. What had caused the loud noise which Rip had heard while coming up the

valley? 4. Did Rip finally taste the liquor which his companion had brought or was he afraid to try it? 5. Was it whiskey or gin which the men drank? 6. Did Rip take more and more of the liquor or did he content himself with one drink? 7. What happened to Rip as he drank more and more of the liquor? 8. What will happen to anyone if he drinks too much liquor? 9. Did Rip at last fall into a deep sleep or into a light sleep? 10. When Rip woke up, was it late afternoon or early morning? 11. Did Rip find a new gun or an old rusty gun beside him when he woke up? 12. Was his dog Wolf still beside him or had Wolf disappeared? 13. When Rip returned to the amphitheatre, was the place just the same or had it changed completely? 14. Did Rip finally start for home very happy or was his heart full of trouble? 15. As he approached the village, did he meet many people whom he knew or many whom he did not recognize?

B. Vocabulary Drill. Choose The Correct Form:

1. *Rusty* means (old, rough, level, corroded).

2. Which of these will make you drunk if you drink much of it (milk, gin, orange juice, tea)?

3. Pick out the silent letters in these words: whistle, listen, answer, knock, knee, whole, wrong.

4. Give sentences, showing clearly the difference in meaning of these four idiomatic phrases: to look at, to look for, to look up, to look out.

5. Give the past tense form and the past participial form of these verbs: swim, rub, excuse, give, hear, begin, make, grow, dare, fall, sleep, think, go, shake. Which of these verbs are "regular verbs" and which are "irregular verbs"?

6. To *make signs to someone* is to (arrest him, make him sign something, motion to him, speak to him).

7. The word *excuse* is pronounced differently when used as a noun than when used as a verb. Distinguish between these two pronunciations.

8. To *approach* something is to (draw back from it, draw near it, shoot at it, fear it).

9. Give the corresponding adjective form of these nouns: hunger, thirst, enthusiasm, difference, rust, height, width, obedience, noise.

10. Explain the difference in meaning between these two sentences: "They stopped *to play* ninepins." and "They stopped *playing* ninepins."

C. Use These In Sentences:

to make signs to, little by little, to fall asleep, to wake up, all night (day), to look for, to play a trick on, to get up, to be filled with, to find out.

PART V

A. Answer These Questions:

1. When Rip came to the edge of the village, did a crowd of strange children or a crowd of familiar children run after him? 2. Did the village appear the same or had it also changed? 3. Were the houses just the same or had many new houses appeared? 4. Did Rip understand all these changes or was he greatly confused by them? 5. Did Rip think that the liquor had made his head more clear or that it had mixed him up badly? 6. When Rip arrived at his own home what did he find? 7. When he called loudly for his wife, did she answer or was there only silence? 8. What new building had replaced the old village inn? 9. What flag was flying from the pole in front of the inn? 10. Did Rip recognize any of the people around the hotel or were they all unknown to him? 11. Did the people of the village show little interest in Rip or did they look at him with great curiosity? 12. Was Rip able to understand their questions or was he greatly confused by their references to voting, elections, politics, etc.? 13. Are all people allowed to vote today in the United States or are there some restrictions as to age, citizenship, etc.? 14. Have women always been allowed to vote in the United States or did they receive the right to vote only recently? 15. Are women permitted to vote in your country?

B. Vocabulary Drill. Choose The Correct Form:

1. If someone is *mixed up,* he is (angry, confused, ill, sleepy).

2. Give the opposites of these words: in front of, old, thin, poor, quiet, empty, question, tall, loudly, before, beautiful, find, bring, dead.

3. Use each of these words in sentences, once as a noun and once as a verb: crowd, question, answer, change, ring, shout, point, head, vote, wish, cause.

4. With which of these words does the contraction *we've* rhyme: live, leave, love, loaf?

5. *Some* eighteen years ago means (*almost* eighteen years ago, *exactly* eighteen years ago, *about* eighteen years ago).

6. The word *drowned* is pronounced to rhyme with (grown, loaned, ruined, found).

7. Use these three idiomatic phrases in sentences, showing clearly the difference in meaning: to call on, to call up, to call for.

8. Distinguish in meaning between: "the roof *fell in*" and "the roof *fell off*."

9. In which of these words is the letter *s* pronounced like *s* and in which is it pronounced like *z*: rusty, dogs, pass, doors, is, was, has, lose, loose, heels, busy?

10. Distinguish in meaning between these pairs of words: pear, pair; heal, heel; bury, berry; passed, past; side, sighed.

C. Use These In Sentences:

to run after, to point at, to bark at, to believe one's eyes, to mix up, to call for, to be gone, to crowd around, to come from, to look for.

PART VI

A. Answer These Questions:

1. Was Rip glad or sad when he heard what had happened to his old friends? 2. Did he understand what the people meant by the word *congress* or was this term new to him? 3. What congress were the people referring to? 4. Of how many houses is the Congress of the United States composed? 5. What was Rip's reaction when he saw his grown son leaning against a tree? 6. Did his son bear little or much resemblance to Rip? 7. Was Rip's son well dressed or poorly dressed? 8. How did Rip reply when someone asked him who he really was? 9. Did the people think that Rip was sane or crazy? 10. Who was the young woman who pushed through the crowd with a child in her arms? 11. What story did this young woman tell about the disappearance of her father? 12. What war had taken place during Rip's absence? 13. Did the Revolutionary War take place in the

17th century or the 18th century? 14. Who was Commander-in-chief of the American Forces during the Revolutionary War? 15. Is the head of the American government known as the Premier or the President?

B. Vocabulary Drill. Choose The Correct Form:

1. *Apparently lazy* means (always lazy, definitely lazy, seemingly lazy, rather lazy).
2. A common synonym for *completely* is (nearly, scarcely, entirely, rarely).
3. Which of the following past tense forms are pronounced as words of one syllable and which are pronounced as words of two syllables: pushed, doubted, died, talked, cried, looked, asked, wanted?
4. The word *knows* is pronounced to rhyme with (news, sews, knees, lose, loose).
5. *Captured* means (recognized, confused, angry, taken prisoner).
6. A synonym for *crazy* is (good-looking, frightened, insane, quiet).
7. Give the full form of these contractions: won't, I'll, don't, wouldn't, he'd, she's, hasn't, weren't, that's been, that's it, it's.
8. In which of these words is the final letter *d* pronounced like *d* and in which is it pronounced like *t*: looked, asked, confused, changed, cried, pushed, talked, awakened, died?
9. With which of these words does the contraction *he'll* rhyme: well, bill, feel, fall?
10. In which of these words is the letter *s* pronounced like *s* and in which is it pronounced like *z*: confuse, dress, knows, what's, he's, years, does, was, changes, ask, vessel, where's?

C. Use These In Sentences:

to be confused by, to talk about, well (poorly) dressed, over there, to fall asleep, to exchange glances, with one another, to get a look at, in order to, to go away.

PART VII

A. Answer These Questions:

1. Was Rip disturbed or comforted by the news of his wife's death? 2. In what manner had Rip's wife died? 3. How long had Rip ac-

tually been absent from the village? 4. How long did he think he had been absent? 5. What do you think really happened to Rip during this long period of absence? 6. Who finally recognized Rip? 7. Did old Peter Vanderdonk finally confirm or deny Rip's story? 8. What did old Peter Vanderdonk have to say about the little men who inhabited the Catskills? 9. With whom did Rip finally go to live? 10. Was Rip now greatly changed in manner or did he soon take up his old walks and customs? 11. Did Rip have much or little interest in matters of government? 12. Did Rip hesitate to mention his story or did he tell it to every stranger that arrived at the hotel? 13. Was his story always the same or did he at first often vary on certain points? 14. Did everyone believe Rip's story or did some people doubt its truth? 15. What do the husbands of the neighborhood often say when they have trouble with their wives?

B. Vocabulary Drill. Choose The Correct Form:

1. A synonym for *hardly* is (with difficulty, scarcely, seldom, frequently).

2. Give the past tense form and the past participial form of these verbs: catch, know, put, tell, seem, think, come, assure, say, play, escape, doubt. Which of these verbs are "regular verbs" and which are "irregular verbs"?

3. The old Dutch game of ninepins, as described in this story, is very similar to present-day (tennis, bowling, soccer, basketball).

4. To *take place* is to (participate, happen or occur, resign, steal or rob).

5. To know something *by heart* is to (forget it, think of it with affection, have learned it by memory, know it for a long time).

6. We use the word *Dutch* to refer to people from (Ireland, Wales, Germany, Holland).

7. Give the corresponding noun form of these adjectives: satisfactory, comfortable, strange, true, poor, free, happy, noisy, long.

8. Distinguish in meaning between *own* used as a verb and *own* used as an adjective.

9. Use each of these words in sentences, once as a noun and once as a verb: doubt, wish, welcome, walk, sleep, interest, matter, escape, trouble, drink.

10. With which of these words does the contraction *we're* rhyme: bear, beer, bore, bar?

C. Use These In Sentences:

at least, to look into, to tell the truth, at once, to make a long story short, to take place, to be interested in, at first, to know something by heart.

Este livro foi impresso na Gráfica Vida e Consciência
sobre papel offset 90g/m² em dezembro de 2007